MECHANICAL TRACTION IN WAR

MECHANICAL TRACTION IN WAR

Lieut-Col OTFRIED LAYRIZ

Translated by R. B. Marston

DAVID & CHARLES REPRINTS

0 7153 6078 7

Printed in Great Britain
by Redwood Press Limited Trowbridge Wiltshire
for David & Charles (Holdings) Limited
South Devon House Newton Abbot Devon

INTRODUCTION TO THE 1973 EDITION

WITH the experience of two great wars behind us, it is easy enough to see that mechanical transport—not to mention the development of armoured fighting vehicles—was bound to become an overwhelming feature of warfare.

But in the 1890s, when Lieut-Col Layriz was writing this book, transport on the roads was attuned largely to the horse, since steam traction had been so badly treated by authority. It is true that steam haulage had been used successfully for forty years, and its use was increasing. As Layriz recounts, it had been featured in a comparatively small way, but with success, in warfare, on military manoeuvres, and experimentally by various governments, but few military minds were far-sighted enough to realise that the future of logistics lay in mechanisation.

Certainly in the Boer War the use of steam traction was in the main highly successful, although still partly experimental. For haulage of heavy guns and stores the big road locomotives could not be beaten, though it should be mentioned that the armour was stripped from the Fowler armoured engines within months of their arrival in Africa. This was probably because it was more of an encumbrance than it was worth—the driver had only two narrow loopholes to look through, and of those the one on the left was by mirror. But the chief advantage may well have been to lose five tons of weight.

In all, between fifty and sixty engines were sent out to the colony for the War Department, but they were augmented appreciably by others requisitioned from haulage firms, mines, and other sources on the spot.

Now let us deal briefly with the story of mechanical military transport after the Boer War. Numerous War Office trials were held during the first few years of the twentieth century, but little or nothing was done to encourage manufacturers of the successful vehicles to develop them further.

A typical case was that of Hornsbys of Grantham in 1908, with a specially built two-cylinder oil-engined vehicle of 70hp, travelling on continuous chain tracks evolved by them. (In passing, and as a matter of interest, the Hornsby-Akroyd oil engine used had been developed from a reliable unit which Hornsbys were producing commercially some five years before Dr Diesel turned out his first viable engine.)

After a highly successful demonstration at the Royal review of 1908, Hornsbys went on to win the War Office Trial first prize of £1,000, with an added bonus of £180 for excellence. The 'caterpillar' tractor, as it was soon christened, was widely acclaimed both in the technical and the lay press, but to no avail. The generals—mostly cavalry officers by training and inclination—preferred their horses to this mechanical contraption. Nor, unfortunately, were civilian orders forthcoming.

To recoup partly their considerable expenditure, Hornsbys sold out the North American patent rights to the Holt Company of New York. In the winter of 1914–15, when the stalemate of trench warfare called for a new type of vehicle to span trenches and to crush barbed-wire entanglements, several Holt caterpillar tractors were imported to try out on this task.

And on the development of that revolutionary vehicle the tank, largely as a result of pressure by Winston Churchill, royalties had to be paid to the Holt Company for the use of what was originally a British invention.

But in World War I mechanical traction and transport were used very extensively. Steam road locomotives were paramount for heavy haulage, including much artillery which was well outside the capacity of any other form of power. Steam tractors were used on lighter haulage work: like the big engines these were principally in the hands of the Royal Engineers and the Royal Artillery. Massive fleets of steam wagons were used by the Army Service Corps. However, it was found that steam vehicles could not be used too near to the front line, because their smoke attracted attention from enemy artillery, and here the petrol lorry and animal transport were in service.

Steam wagons—principally Fodens and Sentinels—were used additionally by the Royal Flying Corps and the Royal Navy, as well as petrol lorries. The Ministry of Munitions used large quantities of mechanical transport to serve the factories, and had a great many steam traction engines for threshing, as well as steam ploughing engines for preparing the land for crop-growing.

One unconventional use for some Foden steam wagons was to fit them up as 'de-lousers', situated near to rest areas. When soldiers came out of the line, their lice-infested clothing was placed on wooden racks in two large steel drums mounted on the wagon platforms, and subjected to steam supplied by the boiler, with effective results.

Many of the vehicles used in World War I were built to special War Department or Ministry of Munitions specification, but others were direct from the augmented production facilities. Even so, demand greatly outstripped supply, and so large numbers were requisitioned, or sometimes hired, from civilian sources.

In World War II, most of the transport was by petrol or diesel vehicles, of course, but on the home front the ability to use home-produced fuel made steam vehicles very valuable, for threshing, ploughing or other farm work: for heavy road haulage: for road construction: for fairground use in keeping up morale: and unusually in pulling down bomb-damaged buildings by use of the winding rope, in London and elsewhere. At some collieries, too, steam plough engines were kept on standby, with extra-long cables on their drums, to act as emergency winding engines in case of pithead bomb damage.

I have told elsewhere how invaluable steam rollers were in the defence of Malta, and of how Fowler ploughing engines were of help in laying 'Pluto', the fuel pipe-line from England to France, beneath the Channel.

The construction of steam road vehicles had virtually ceased in the 1930s, of course, but in 1940 Marshalls and Ransomes each built two traction engines for the Ministry, and up to 1944 Marshalls built over twenty steam rollers. So far as is known, these were the last steam vehicles built anywhere for war purposes.

W. J. HUGHES

Tytherington
Macclesfield

MECHANICAL TRACTION IN WAR

FIG. 1*a*.—ANOTHER 'FOREIGN DEVIL': HOW THE KAFFIRS VIEW THE ALDERSHOT TRACTION ENGINES IN SOUTH AFRICA.

The travelling traction engines from Aldershot frighten the Kaffirs terribly. Frequently they take a party of natives unawares, and the sight of the monsters and the shrill noise of their whistles scatters them in all directions. I have to thank the Proprietors of the *Daily Graphic* for the use of this illustration.—TRANSLATOR.

[*Frontispiece.*

MECHANICAL TRACTION IN WAR

FOR ROAD TRANSPORT

WITH NOTES ON AUTOMOBILES GENERALLY

BY

LIEUT.-COL. OTFRIED LAYRIZ

OF THE GERMAN ARMY

TRANSLATED BY R. B. MARSTON

'. . . The value of steam traction as an efficient supplement to animal transport, especially in carrying supplies in rear of an army, was clearly proved.'—*Report on the Salisbury Manœuvres*, 1898, *from* FIELD-MARSHAL RIGHT HON. LORD WOLSELEY, K.P., ETC., COMMANDER-IN-CHIEF, *to the Secretary of State for War.*

ILLUSTRATED

LONDON

SAMPSON LOW, MARSTON AND COMPANY

LIMITED

St. Dunstan's House

FETTER LANE, FLEET STREET, E.C.

1900

Edinburgh : T. and A. CONSTABLE, Printers to Her Majesty

PREFACE

The transport of food and war material from the terminus of the railway to the camp is of the utmost importance to the army, and calls for the employment of all available means. Road transport by means of mechanical traction is now so developed as to be worthy of serious consideration in conjunction with horse traction for war purposes, and for this reason an attempt to set out the possibilities offered by various methods of mechanical traction may be justified.

THE AUTHOR.

TRANSLATOR'S NOTE

Being greatly interested in the use of the traction engine and other automobiles in war, I am glad to present English and American military officers and engineers with an English edition of this, as I venture to think, most valuable and suggestive work by Lieutenant-Colonel Layriz.

I have added some footnotes, and references in the Appendix to the use of the traction engine in the South African War, etc., also an account of the Thousand Mile Motor Car Trial, which, under the auspices of the Automobile Club, has recently taken place with such striking success.

To the illustrations I have added the interesting pictures of early road engines and carriages,—the forerunners of the great automobile army now coming into existence in all parts of the world.

By the courtesy of the proprietors of the *Daily Graphic* I have been able to give some illustrations of the armoured road train recently ordered by Lord Roberts.

R. B. MARSTON.

LIST OF ILLUSTRATIONS

CONTENTS

I

INTRODUCTION

II

HISTORY OF MECHANICAL TRACTION

III

THE AUTOMOBILE WITHOUT TRAIN

IV

THE AUTOMOBILE AS TRACTION ENGINE

V

A MOTOR CAR WHICH CAN BE USED BOTH AS AUTOMOBILE AND FOR TRACTION

VI

ATTEMPTS TO REPLACE THE STEAM MOTOR BY OTHER KINDS OF MOTORS

VII

RELATION OF SUPPLY TRANSPORT BY MEANS OF TRACTION ENGINES TO THAT BY FIELD RAILWAYS

VIII

MECHANICAL ROAD TRACTION MUST BE GENERAL IN A COUNTRY BEFORE IT CAN BE USEFULLY EMPLOYED IN WAR TIME

APPENDIX

RÉSUMÉ OF EXPERIMENTS IN MECHANICAL TRACTION WITH ROAD LOCOMOTIVES FOR WAR PURPOSES

MECHANICAL TRACTION IN WAR

I

INTRODUCTION

THE question of the adaptability of mechanical traction for use in war is of the greatest interest; and the important part played by the railway in modern campaigns is well known, but it by no means exhausts the use of mechanical power for war transport purposes. The increasing size of armies has necessitated still further substitution of mechanical for animal traction.

Mechanical Traction a necessity.

Already in 1870 it was found that the means of transport for war material for the German army was deficient; but the disadvantages were not so much felt, as the army was operating in a densely populated country, and its victories enabled it to extend the district from which it drew its supplies in advancing. Forced contributions sufficient for feeding large bodies of troops in future wars cannot be relied on, as they will certainly fail if the operations are arrested for strategic purposes; for instance, before fortifications, or if armies have to alter their line of march and concentrate, as in the case of Sedan.[1]

Reserve Supplies as well as Requisitions necessary.

Another reason for reform in army transport methods is the fact that the field force of the present day must use heavy guns in carrying out the duties assigned to it; such guns as formerly were only required by troops engaged in

[1] Schäffer, *Der Kriegstrain des deutschen Herres*, 1897, p. 80.

Mechanical Traction for bringing up Guns against Sperrforts, Fortified Positions, or Entrenchments.

siege operations. In some cases it depends on the effect of these guns, especially their timely action against barrier forts,[1] whether an army must fight in its own country, or can do so in that of the enemy. For bringing up such guns, their ammunition, platforms, etc., automobile traction engines may be of the greatest value; and after bringing their loads to the place where they are required, they can be converted into stationary engines for hauling loads across country by means of wire ropes, thus accelerating the work of arming the batteries for action.

Too late to arrange for Mechanical Traction when War begins.

Mechanical traction for traffic has, during the last hundred years, made undreamt-of advances towards perfection. But its development is not yet complete. To wait until perfection is arrived at, as recommended in some quarters, is not expedient for the army. Such a policy may, in case of war, deprive the army entirely, or to a great extent, of important aid. And experience proves that an invention or appliance is of no use to an army in war time unless it has got acquainted with it and accustomed to it in peace time.

Previous to 1870 Germany was behind other countries in matters connected with the subject of this work. Native industries gave the German army no encouragement to experiment with road traction engines. The use of these engines, imported from England, was improvised during the

[1] Barrier forts (sperrforts). That invaluable work, Brockhaus's *Konverzation's Lexikon*, gives the following description of what the Germans call sperrforts (TRANSLATOR):—

'Sperrforts, isolated forts intended to bar the way of an invading army at points where it can best be done (river and mountain defiles). Themselves secure from surprise, and being carried by storm, they should be capable of holding out in proportion to the length of time it would take an invader to make a way round. They should compel the invader to use heavy artillery in attacking them, and be armed with heavy guns in iron casemates and iron cupolas, and provided with bomb-proof chambers and galleries for the protection of the garrison. Noteworthy are the forts of this description in the Italian, Austrian, Swiss, and French Alps, built to defend the passes; also the chain of barrier forts in France on the Moselle and Saar.'

Franco-German war. As a consequence, the results achieved with them were not at all equal to their capabilities, even at that time.

There should be no Technical Improvisations in War!

Improvised effort almost always ends in failure. As a contrast to the traction engine may be mentioned the air balloon. Whereas their war balloons rendered the French important services, the Germans were unable to use the only balloon they had, one obtained during the war from England for the purpose of observing the artillery fire from Strasburg.

It is time, then, to recognise the necessity for preparing beforehand and in peace time for the proper use of the traction engine in war. It is also necessary that this recognition should become general among the people, for sooner or later their representatives will be asked to supply the money required for the purpose. The nation must be prepared for as great an outlay on traction engines and plant as the rearmament of the infantry has hitherto cost. Germany grudges no expenditure on arms. Since it is now a question of equally great expenditure on means of military transport, the government and people should not forget that they owe the victories of 1870 to the circumstance that Prussia made timely use of the invention of the railway and telegraph (and the facilities afforded by them for more rapid transport) in the formation of strategic lines.

Cost of creating Mechanical Traction Plant.

At the present time explosion or detonating motors or electric motors are to the front, and they come to mind first when it is a question of mechanical traction. But one must be on guard against the attractions of the sensational. These modern automobiles are not yet suited for the transport of heavy loads for war purposes—even with not illiberal allowances as regards cost and simplicity. War does not concern itself with the beautiful and intellectual invention. How small was the damage done to the Germans in 1870 by the technically highly interesting Mitrailleuse; and how little hurt were the French by the no less ingenious Feldl quick-firing machine.[1] Before a scientific novelty can be of use in war, under conditions often of extraordinary difficulty, it must have been thoroughly well tested in every possible way in peace time.

The Locomotive is also an Automobile, and useful in War.

But it is quite another matter when the question of mechanical traction refers to the locomotive, which, of course, is also an automobile. Of its use *on rails* it is needless to say a word. But on roads *without rails* it can also be of the greatest use in military transport. This is still disputed. The road locomotive does not shine as a pacemaker, and in this respect compares poorly with the railway engine or the express benzine automotor. All the same, the army traction engine's pace, in its place *behind* the troops, is quite sufficient, and its day's work is worth at least double that obtainable with animal traction.

[1] Used by the Bavarian army in 1870.

FIG. 1.—Cugnot's Locomotive, 1769.

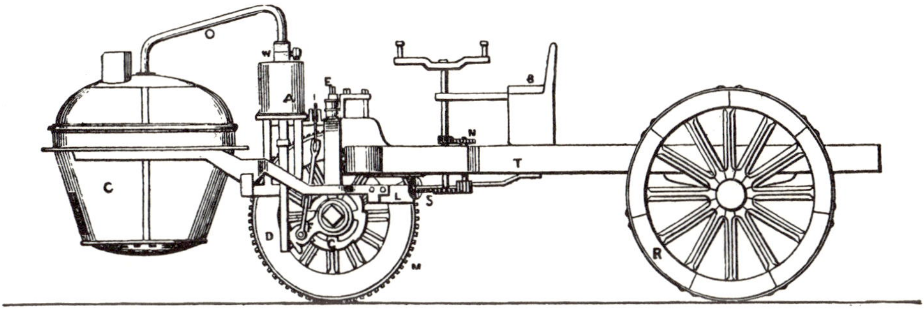

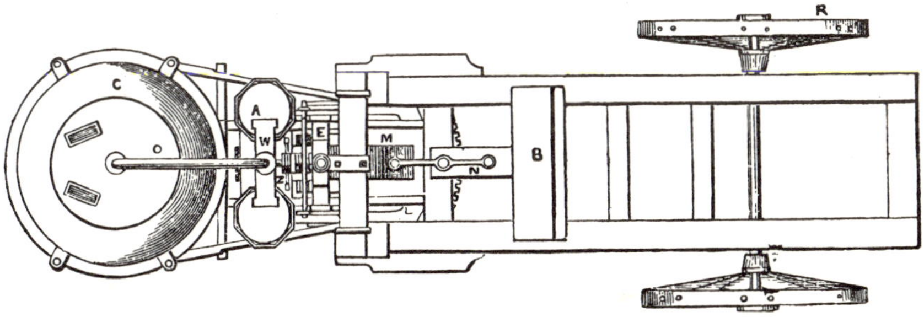

FIG. 2.—Cugnot's Locomotive Carriage, 1769. Fig. 1. Elevation. Fig. 2. Plan.

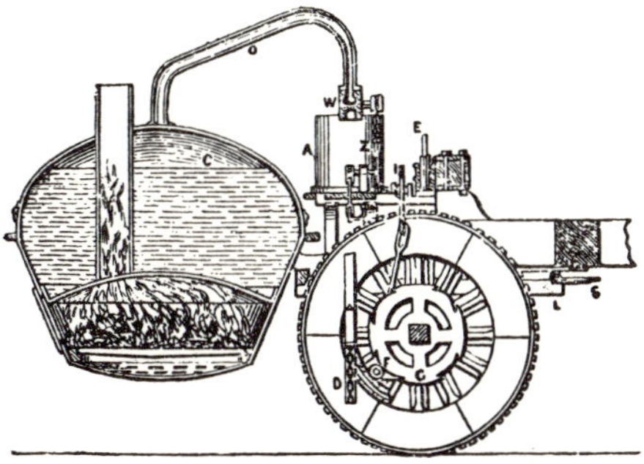

FIG. 3.—Longitudinal Section of Front Part of Cugnot's Engine.

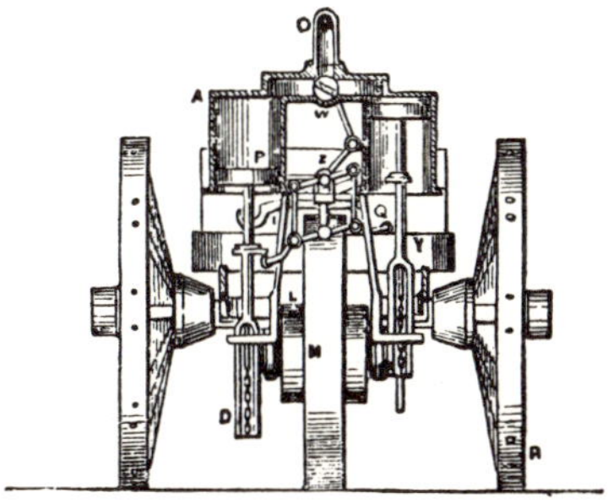

FIG. 4.—Transverse Section of Cugnot's Engine.

To Nicholas Joseph Cugnot (born at Void, in Lorraine, Feb. 26, 1729; died at Paris, 1804) belongs the credit of having first constructed a carriage whose wheels were propelled by steam. In 1769 he made an engine to run on common roads which was moved by two single-acting cylinders, whose pistons acted alternately on the single front wheel.

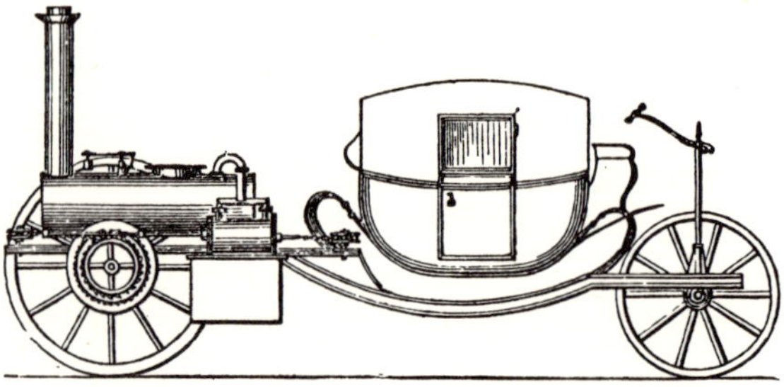

Fig. 5.—William Symington's Steam Carriage, 1786.

Symington's steam carriage is said to have worked very efficiently. He used the condenser and ratchet motion similar to that used by him in the steamboat, of which, it has been claimed, he was the original inventor.

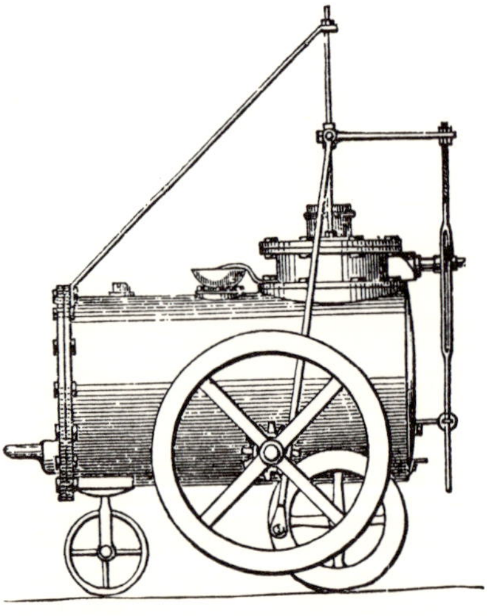

Fig. 6.—Trethvick and Vivian's Engine, 1802.

In 1802 Messrs. Trethvick and Vivian invented a combined high pressure engine and boiler, which may be considered the forerunner of our present locomotives.

In 1772 Oliver Evans, an American wheelwright, began to experiment in making steam wagons, etc., but the first vehicle of any kind which he appears to have used was in 1804, when he made a river lighter, driven by a 5 horse-power engine, and afterwards put wheels to it and ran it on land.

II

HISTORY OF MECHANICAL TRACTION [1]

The Road Traction Engine the Forerunner of the Railway Engine.

SINCE the locomotive is included in the consideration of military mechanical traction, a brief review of the development of transport by means of traction engines may be given.

With the insufficient means of a still undeveloped technical knowledge, the problem of mechanical traction was again attacked at the beginning of the nineteenth century, and the idea, which originated in the previous century, of utilising steam for driving engines was further developed. The construction of steam carriages for use on country roads engaged the attention of inventors in England, the native land of Watt [2] and Stephenson.

Early Difficulties of Road Traction Engines in England.

The introduction of the giant road-engine, which ruined the roads, damaged the bridges, and scared the horses, met with great opposition from the authorities, and the promoters of traffic by means of these new-fashioned vehicles found themselves compelled to build special roads for them.

[1] Probably the best work dealing with this subject up to the year 1860 is a now scarce work, entitled, '*The Economy of Steam Power on Common Roads*, in relation to Agriculturists, Railway and Canal Companies, Mine and Coal Owners, Quarry Proprietors, Contractors, etc., with its History and Practice in Great Britain. By Charles F. T. Young, C.E.: and Its Progress in the United States. By A. L. Holley, C.E., and J. K. Fisher. With Engravings by J. H. Rimbault.' Among the illustrations is one of the Griffiths Steam Road Coach (1821), the first of the kind constructed in England expressly for the conveyance of passengers on common roads. I have taken this illustration and several others from this work.—TRANSLATOR.

[2] Watt was a Scotsman.—TRANSLATOR.

They combined with them rail tracks, as it had been proved that with the reduced friction the steam traction engine could be used economically.

With the Development of Railways the Road Engine is forgotten.

Then for a long period the whole energy of the most distinguished engineers of the time, and the capital of the country were employed in establishing railways. It was not until the fifties that the question of the employment of steam locomotives on ordinary roads again came to the front in England, in order to utilise them for the transport of heavy goods on country roads, and thus restrict the extension of costly railroads. The further development of this kind of locomotive was even carried so far as to permit of attempts to construct them for across-country work.[1]

New Departure in the Evolution of the Road Locomotive growing out of the Locomobile Engine.

When social conditions in England necessitated the employment of machinery in agricultural work, the engines required were at first constructed to be moved from place to place by horse-power, and later, like railway locomotives, were self-propelling.[2]

Attempts in cross-country Engine-driving.

Then, for a considerable time, attempts were made to substitute steam-power for horse-power in ploughing, by harnessing a locomotive to the plough in place of the horse. For this purpose the engine must be light enough not to sink too deeply into soft ground. But it was soon recognised as a law of steam-power, that the more freely the power concentrated in an engine can be used, the greater is the

[1] That this was no visionary dream has been proved by the work of our military traction engines in the present war in South Africa. I have to thank the proprietors of the *Daily Graphic* for the illustration (see *Frontispiece*) by one of their war artists of the startling effect on the Kaffirs of a traction engine and train rolling—one might almost say rollicking—over the veldt.—TRANSLATOR.

[2] Boydell, Patent Specification No. 11,357 of August 29, 1846. For an account of the Boydell Engine see *Parliamentary Papers*, Ordnance Select Committees, of 25th June 1858. The engine is also described in the *Engineer*, Nos. 82 and 136.

amount of work which can be got out of it, and this notwithstanding the fact that its size, weight, and cost of installation may be increased thereby. So the system of harnessing the engine to draw the plough after itself across the field was abandoned in favour of the stationary ploughing engine, by means of wire-rope and drum (clipdrum-system).[1]

First Use of Traction Engine in War (see Fig. 10).

The earlier of these forms of steam-ploughs (engine harnessed to the plough) gave rise to the first use of the road locomotive for the transport of heavy artillery, and this was by the English army during the Crimean war;[2] but during the following long period of peace, and owing to the excessive extent to which economy was practised in military circles, the traction engine found no admirers.

In England, on the other hand, great factories were established for the production of steam ploughs, steam road-rollers, and steam road locomotives. As absurdly stringent official regulations hindered their use in England, they found their principal market in the Colonies.[3]

Failure of the Road Locomotive in Germany.

Through the London Exhibition of 1862, the attention of Germany was attracted to the road locomotive. German factories now began to build them, and obtained prizes at German agricultural shows. In 1863 in the Palatinate experiments for the purpose of testing the endurance of road-locomotives in drawing heavy goods took place, but failed entirely in consequence of want of perseverance on the part of the makers in overcoming the many glaring defects in their engines. Moreover, at that time the want of more rapid road transport in country districts had not made itself felt in Germany.

The conditions have changed since then. There has been a gradual withdrawal of the population from the agricultural

[1] Eyth, *Wanderbuch eines Ingenieurs*, 1871. Appendix 1 and 2.
[2] Rühlmann, *Maschinenlehre*: Brunswick, 1867, p. 138.
[3] Hansard, *Parliamentary Debates*, 1857-58, July 30.

Shall Branch Lines or Automobile Road Traction supplement Main Line Traffic?

districts. Manufacturing industries, long confined to the great towns, have gone into the country, where they find cheaper labour, often their raw materials to hand, and can use water-power to the best advantage. This means dependence on goods traffic with the trade centres. The existence of agriculture and of manufactures carried on in country districts depends directly on the perfection of means of transport. Animal traction is too expensive in this case, canal systems are wanting, and for many kinds of goods water transport is too slow. One is faced, then, by the problem whether the main railway lines shall be connected by a widely extended network of branch lines, or whether the cheaper, automobile road train, more suited to small requirements, should be made use of.

Transport on rails does not meet all requirements. As the metal rails cannot follow all the bends and ups and downs of a country road, in many cases a regular railroad like the main line must be built, so that the expense of the branch line is often as great. The laying down of rails on country roads upsets the general traffic to some extent, and therefore requires the assent of the highest authorities (Parliamentary powers, as we say in England). Thus the need for quicker and yet railless transport has of late given a renewed impetus to the development of mechanical traction.

Since the invention of the Lenoir gas engine[1] (1860) various methods of constructing motors have been discovered; used at first for small power auxiliary stationary engines, they proved later to be suitable for driving vehicles.

Apart from the fact that the war of 1870 affected, prejudicially, the development of this new industry, it was again shown that rail lines, not in this case for connecting towns with towns, but as tramways for more rapid communications between the larger towns and their suburbs and manu-

[1] Musil, *Die Motoren für Gewerbe und Industrie*: Brunswick, 1887, p. 105.

The Development of Tramways hindered the Introduction of Automobiles not running on Rails.

facturing quarters, attracted all the enterprise of the capitalists. It was not until 1886, when the German engineer, Daimler,[1] succeeded in constructing his explosion-motor[2] that it was possible to run vehicles at high speeds on good roads. Since then, France setting the example, there has been a rapidly growing movement in favour of mechanical traction, a movement which has attained such proportions that already we hear talk—certainly much exaggerated—of the coming of the horseless age.

[1] Lieckfeld, *Die Petroleum und Benzinmotoren*: Munich, 1894, p. 49.

[2] The following brief account of the Daimler Motor is from Lockert's *Petroleum Motor Cars*. London: Sampson Low, Marston & Co. (TRANSLATOR):—

'The Daimler engine acts in four stages or cycles. The first cycle is the period of the charging stroke, during which the explosive compound supplied by the gas-inlet enters the cylinder through a valve, and is mixed with a considerable quantity of air. . . . In the second cycle or period of compression the piston compresses the compound in the cylinder. Ignition is effected by means of an incandescent tube heated by a fixed burner. The third cycle, subsequent to the ignition, is the period of the useful stroke, while the fourth is the period of the return stroke of the piston during which the burnt gases are expelled.'

For full illustrated description of automobiles of all kinds, including the latest American traction engines, fire engines, motor cars, etc., see *Horseless Vehicles, Automobiles, and Motor Cycles*. By Gardiner D. Hiscox, M.E. London: Sampson Low, Marston & Co. Every one interested in Automobiles should possess a copy of *The Automotor and Horseless Vehicle Pocket-Book of Automotive Formulæ*, published by Messrs. F. King & Co., Ltd., 62 St. Martin's Lane, E.C.—TRANSLATOR.

III

THE AUTOMOBILE WITHOUT TRAIN

Experiments with Light, Rapid Automobiles.

THE development of motors driven by one of the naphtha hydrocarbons (petrol, benzine, gasoline, etc.) is still in its infancy. Not until 1892 was it proved by experiments, carried out in France, that such automotor vehicles could be driven, not only on well-kept streets, but also on ordinary country roads, and at a pace which allowed of competition with the railway mail train service.

Experiments with Automobiles for Heavy Loads.

This encouraged the attempt to utilise these motors in the construction of large automotor vehicles for the transport of heavy loads. And these attempts opened the way for competition among all kinds of engines adapted for mechanical traction. The builders of steam engines entered the lists with new models, which in England have so far won the day over the explosion motors, in that they alone have succeeded in fulfilling the stipulated conditions as regards power, endurance, and control.[1]

Justification of Attempts to introduce Mechanical Traction generally.

The endeavour, so marked at the present time, to replace animal by mechanical traction on roads, is looked upon by many as a fad or folly of the day, whereas it is in reality a link in the chain of endeavour which connects the end of the century with its commencement.

[1] For a full illustrated account of these 'explosion' or 'detonating' motors, see *Petroleum Motor Cars*. By M. Louis Lockert. London: Sampson Low, Marston & Company. M. Lockert has also published excellent little works in French on *Steam Motor Cars* and *Motor Cars worked by Electricity, Compressed Air, etc.*—TRANSLATOR.

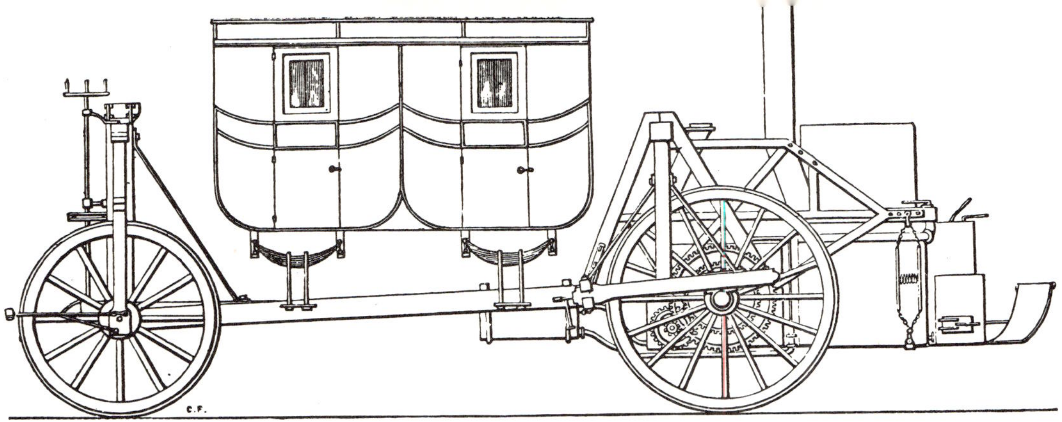

Fig. 7.—Griffiths' Steam Coach, 1821. The first made in England for passenger traffic on roads.

[Griffiths was the first to use the water tube system for his boiler, as now used in the Belleville and Serpollet systems.—Translator.]

Hancock's steam coach ran many hundreds of miles very successfully. It carried four passengers, and was propelled by a pair of oscillating cylinders, working the double cranked axle of the front, or steering wheel.

Fig. 8.—Walter Hancock's Three-Wheeled Steam Coach, 1828.

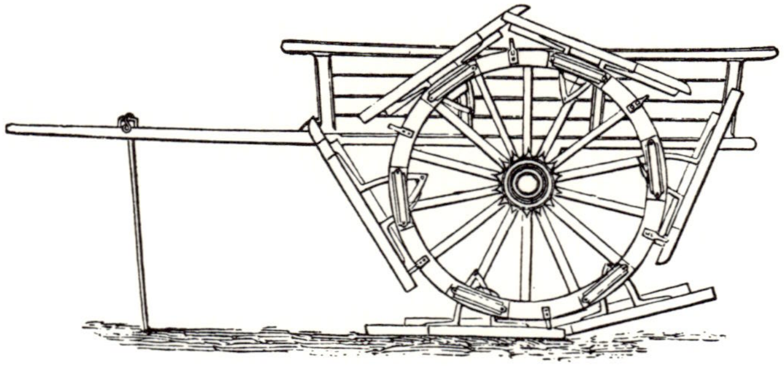

Fig. 9.—Cart fitted with Boydell's 'Endless Rails,' 1855.

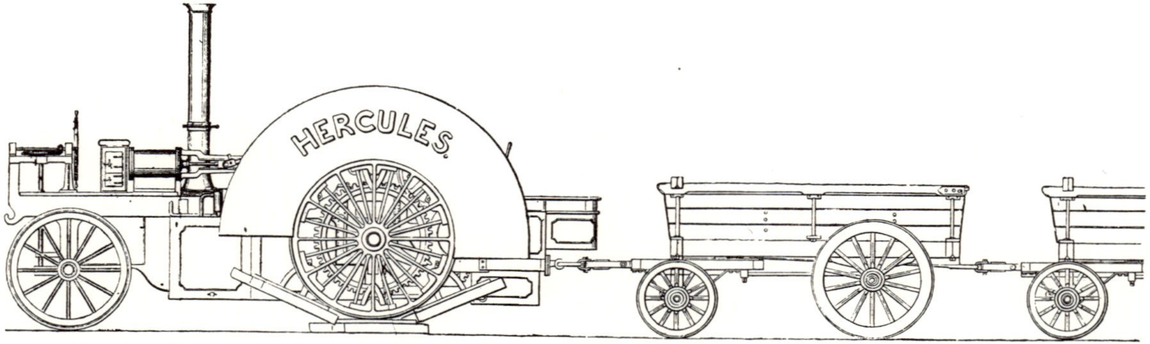

Fig. 10.—The Boydell Traction Engine with Endless Rails (*Porte Rail*), 1854. As used in Crimean War.

The Exigencies of War the Standard of Utility as regards Employment of Mechanical Traction with an Army.

In attempting to deal with the problem of selecting among different systems of mechanically driven vehicles such as may be suitable for military use, it is necessary to ascertain perfectly clearly the conditions under which the transport of heavy material is effected in war.

From this point of view an attempt will be made to describe the various methods of transport which are possible at the present time by means of mechanical traction (*i.e.* with engines of some kind in contradistinction to animal traction with horses, mules, oxen, etc.).

Importance of the Daimler Motor in the development of Light Automobile Vehicles.

Oil-motors are a development of the gas-burning engines used in small industries,—they are also gas-motors, but on the explosion principle. The necessary quantity of gas is conducted into the carburettor and there mixed with atmospheric air; this explosive gas mixture is fired at the moment when the motor piston passes the dead point. In the so-called four-cycle explosion motors one stroke of the piston in the cylinder corresponds with two turns of the driving shaft.

In 1885 the German engineer Daimler substituted the incandescent tube lighter for the open flame ignition method used in stationary motors. It was now for the first time possible to construct fast road-motors of comparatively light weight (40 kg. (=80 lbs.) per horse-power). With small consumption of fuel (0·42 kg. benzine (not quite 1 lb.) per hour and horse-power) they could also now be used for vehicles (including boats). Complications with horse traffic arising out of the mechanism of motive power were unavoidable.

To overcome the resistances in the machine required the storage of power in a fly-wheel capable of from 1500 to as much in some cases as 2000 revolutions per minute. But with shaft and piston driven at such speed it was necessary to provide special arrangements for cooling the cylinder jacket, and running the axles in oil baths. The velocity of the fly-wheel and driving crank required some plan of reduced speed for transmission to the axles of the driving wheels. The great distance of the driving wheels from the motor necessitated an intermediate axle, on which are arranged driving drums graded for different speeds, and varying in form according as the transmission of rotation is effected by means of cog-wheels or chain.

The steering arrangements necessitate differential gearing, and of special importance are the arrangements for working the brakes, for running backwards, and for preventing the machine running backwards when stopped on a hillside.

After the incandescent tube the electric spark was also used for igniting the gas used for driving motor cars on the exploding or detonating method; ignition by means of magnetic induction was also tried. But the use of electricity necessitates batteries, accumulators, or a small motor-driven dynamo.

Is the Incandescent Tube or Electric Ignition preferable?

Successful working of the motor depends chiefly on the ignition of the gas mixture at the proper moment. Electric ignition is too complicated for use in war, and presupposes the possibility of recharging the batteries and accumulators. With gases derived from petroleum ignition by electric spark is not to be relied on. With electric ignition benzine gas could alone be employed, which, on account of its dangerously inflammable nature, can only be used to a limited extent for vehicles used in war. Escape of benzine through carelessness or leakage may give rise to explosions, since benzine evaporates at ordinary temperatures, and the gas mixed with atmospheric air is highly explosive.

Danger of Benzine as Fuel.

Benzine motors can be used perfectly well in vehicles (*Fahrzeuge*) not intended for war purposes. In such cases the reservoirs can be filled up with the greatest care, and, whenever possible, only by daylight. In war, when marching often occupies the whole of the day, there is no alternative but to replenish the store of benzine at night with a naked or at best badly protected light.

Drawbacks in use of Petroleum.

For these reasons military vehicles have to fall back on petroleum, although, apart from its unpleasant smell, it causes soot accumulations which choke the valves, necessitating constant cleaning, and the incandescent method of ignition which must be used with it is not unsusceptible to weather influences.[1] Petroleum is subject to price fluctuations, and in this respect the competition between Russian and American supplies is advantageous to the consumer.[2] In Germany in 1894 the price of benzine, duty free in barrels, was 16 marks 75 pfennings (16s. 9d.) per kilogram (=2 lbs.). At the present time, since the opening up of the Danube navigation (by blasting at the Iron Gates) up to Regensburg, the greater facilities for competition afforded to Russian petroleum will probably still further reduce the price of benzine.

Use of Spirit.

The possibility of substituting home-made spirit for benzine and petroleum (in the interests of home industries) has been considered. But it appears certain that spirit cannot be produced cheaply enough. All the same, it is worth noting that we are not entirely dependent on foreign sources for the necessary gas-producing material.

Importance of the Rubber Tyre in Motor Carriages.

Rubber tyres are necessary in the construction of light and rapid motor carriages. Even on the best roads a rapidly driven motor carriage is liable to jolts and shocks, and it is only by using rubber tyres that injury to delicate machinery can be avoided or greatly lessened. The cost of rubber is considerable, and its use necessitates larger and more expensive rims to the wheels, whether for ordinary or pneumatic tyres. Rubber tyre wheels are also expensive because the rubber loses its elasticity under the effects of great heat and cold; it perishes, and soon becomes useless.

Recently it appears to have been found possible to lessen

[1] There is no smell or smoke from the 'Motor-Car' spirit sold by the Anglo-American Oil Company (specific gravity, 0·680). See account of the 1000 mile motor trial in the Appendix.—TRANSLATOR.

[2] *Handels-Revue*, vi. No. 4, 31st January 1899.

the effects of wear and tear on rough roads. In Simms' patent there is a thick indiarubber tread which is so made as to be detachable when worn, when it can be replaced easily. Messrs. Simms have fitted a motor gun-carriage with their patent compound pneumatic tyre (see *The Automobile* for June 1899).

Very few substitutes for rubber exist at present, so that a reduction in price is not to be expected, especially as patents threatening their monopoly are bought up by the rubber manufacturers.

Even for motor carriages intended for carrying heavy weights, rubber tyres are necessary, as they permit a heavy weight to be carried with less waste of power than ordinary tyres.[1]

Explosion motor carriages are constructed in various forms. Very light two- and three-wheelers, and light and heavy four-wheelers, 30 kg. (60 lbs.). Two-wheelers for one person have already been constructed, of from 1 to 4 horse-power; also two-wheelers for two persons (tandems). Motor three-wheelers, weighing from 70 to 80 kg. (140 to 160 lbs.), are used chiefly for sporting purposes. In France the good state of the roads has deluded the military authorities into the adaptation of three-wheelers for army purposes. But these machines, from the very nature of their construction, can never be serviceable for military purposes, as on bad streets and ordinary country roads with ruts they are useless. Light 240 lbs. four-wheel motors for two persons, and of from 4 to 6 horse-power, are to be had, and are considered in America to be suitable as Maxim gun carriages (see Fig. 13). For military purposes four-wheel carriages are best constructed with two independent motors, which can be worked together or singly; but this necessitates heavy machines. Carriages of this kind, with motors up to

[1] All interested in heavy traffic should see the 'Roller Bearing' Company's exhibit at the Crystal Palace.—TRANSLATOR.

15 horse-power, have been constructed to carry sixteen to eighteen persons (as omnibus), or a load up to five tons (as freight wagons).

Various suggestions have been made for the employment for army purposes in war time of the different kinds of automobiles not intended for drawing a train of wagons.

For instance, it is suggested to employ for courier service the light motor cars which are used in motor car races, and which with an average speed of 24 km. (14 to 15 miles) under favourable conditions on good level roads have done 30, 40, and even 50 km. in the hour (up to 27 or 28 miles). But it is questionable whether results such as these (attained in peace time under exceptional conditions) will be possible in war, when the roads are encumbered with troops and impedimenta of all kinds, and in thickly populated districts and in unknown countries. Moreover, there should be no illusion that map studying and taking one's bearings can be done without stopping, for the high speed makes it impossible to read a map or use a field-glass, even if one is not occupied in guiding the car. All the same the motor car will, in the long-run, get over more ground in the day than the horse-rider or cyclist can.

Has the Courier Service the same importance as formerly?

In Napoleon's time the courier service with relays of horses, *à franc étrier*, was the chief means of transmitting diplomatic dispatches and army orders, and that, too, over such distances for instance as from Paris to Moscow or Madrid,[1] and there is no reason why a similar means of communication should not be of the greatest service at the present day at some decisive moment, when the ordinary railway communications are interrupted or do not exist. But under ordinary conditions the field telegraph does away with the services of couriers, so that it is not likely there will ever be any extended use of motor cars for such purposes.

[1] *Mémoires du Général Baron de Marbot*: Paris, 1891.

Transport of Ammunition and Wounded.

The use of light motor carriages for the transport of ammunition and the wounded may be possible in the future. At present they are not suited for this purpose, as they are not constructed for work other than on roads.

Motor freight wagons as already used by breweries, furniture removal businesses, etc., in towns, can be used for military purposes (fig. 14). It is simply a question in this case of cost of mechanical as compared with horse power. If it is cheaper, it will find such extended employment that the army can rely on it for the establishment of supply columns. They must be taken as they are, and used to the best advantage possible.

But if it is a question of creating types of motor freight cars, specially adapted for use in train formation for ammunition, commissariat, and baggage transport for an army in the field, the possibility that animal draught may be necessary must always be kept in view. For this reason the wagons must not be too heavy, though this may necessitate less carrying capacity than is the case with motor freight cars not specially constructed for army use. In non-military motor freight cars the utmost advantage must be taken of the fact that with a powerful motor, heavier loads can be carried than by means of an ordinary two-horse wagon. In this case the object in view is greater money-earning power, and whereas an ordinary motor freight car may be constructed to carry five tons, that specially intended for military use must not be built to carry more than a ton or a ton and a half.

Use as Kitchen and Tool Wagons.

The employment of motor kitchen cars, which has also been suggested, is not worth consideration. It would be of more consequence to so construct the tool cars (*werkzeugwagen*) of the pioneer detachments of cavalry divisions, that they could be either driven by a motor or drawn by horses.

The only really felt want for the automotor is as light

The Cycle Corps and Light Motor Cars.

baggage carriers to accompany the cycle corps, whose employment for independent service is only possible in conjunction with them. Supplies of ammunition, surgical bandages, maps, etc., can be carried by their means as quickly as the average pace of the cycle corps requires.

It is of the greatest importance that officers of the general staff sent to some distant point under protection of a cyclist detachment should be able to cover the ground without too much fatigue, so that when their work of reconnoitring and sending written dispatches begins they may come fresh to it.

Experiments with Light Automobiles.

Experiences with automobile vehicles as such (*i.e.* not used for drawing carriages) are too few to give much clue to their value for military purposes. Competitions between such vehicles were encouraged in the French press in 1892, and a race which took place on the 6th and 7th of March 1898, between Marseilles and Nice,[1] is noteworthy from the fact that on one of the days the weather was fine and the roads in good order, and on the other wet and the roads bad. The average pace established, even for bad weather, was 25 to 30 kilometres (about 15 to 20 miles) per hour for light four-wheel automobiles, for motocycles (three- and two-wheelers) only 20 kilometres (12 to 13 miles). As one is inclined to consider light two- and three-wheelers as faster than four-wheelers, this result is striking. But the explanation is a perfectly natural one, viz., that driving a two- or three-wheeler over slippery roads requires great care, whereas the four-wheeler can be driven at the higher speeds even under such conditions.

The two-wheeler has probably a wider field of utility before it, although at present scarcely answering all requirements. The three-wheeler alone is unsuited for military use; it takes up as much width on the road as the four-wheeler,

[1] *France Militaire*, 28th January 1898 and 15th April 1898.

but with its three-wheel track is unable to avoid the bad places so well.

Experiments with Heavy Automobiles.

Races have also taken place between heavier automobiles, which have proved that they can be run at a very considerable pace on good roads. But experiments under military conditions, *i.e.* such as exist in war time, are wanting, these consist specially in the necessity for a long train of vehicles following close one after another. Collisions may arise in consequence of differences in the pace of the column, caused for example by the head of the column being retarded at the commencement of a steep incline, whilst the rest of it still on level ground keeps up its pace. In consequence of the long duration of the march, especially when it takes place at night, the nerves of the drivers get overtaxed. It remains to be seen whether the acetylene light, which is recommended for other military purposes, such as searching the battlefield for wounded, will be so improved for lighting vehicles as to be perfectly reliable. Without some such system of lighting the wagons or other vehicles must be kept far apart and the pace greatly moderated.

Keeping the Roads clear at Night an absolute necessity.

This question, and that of keeping the roads clear at night, and many others, must be answered by actual experiment under such conditions as obtain in war time, before any decision can be arrived at as to the value of automobile vehicles for transport of heavy loads in war.

See 'Harmsworth's Magazine,' April 1900, *for interesting illustrated articles on 'The* 1000 *Mile Motor Race,' and 'The Cycle as Ambulance.'*

I have given some account of the great race at the end of this work. The value of 'Petrol' has been thoroughly established; in its best forms it is smokeless, odourless, and cheap. The ignition question appears not likely to present any grave difficulties in future.—TRANSLATOR.

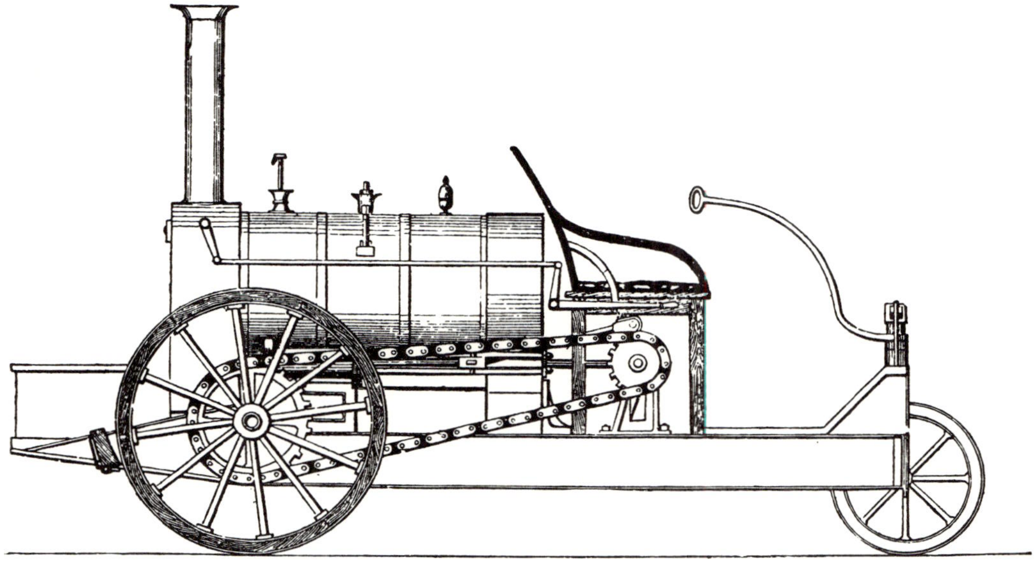

FIG. 11.—The Marquis of Stafford's Steam Coach (weight under 1 ton), 1859.

[The sprocket-wheel and chain action is interesting in view of the revolution its use in the bicycle made.—TRANSLATOR.]

The Engineer, in noticing the doings of this little engine, says: 'On Monday last (March 7, 1859), Lord Stafford and party made another trip from Buckingham to Wolverton. His lordship drove and steered; and although the roads from constant rain were very heavy, they were not more than an hour in running the nine miles to Wolverton.' It was so easy to guide, that Lord Sefton drove it several miles the first time he rode on it; at a speed of one mile in five minutes its action was perfectly steady. It appears to have had accommodation for four passengers, as on one occasion the Marquis of Stafford drove Lord Alfred Paget and two Hungarian noblemen on it. It weighed 2134 lbs. light, and 3360 lbs. loaded, consumed 6 to 7 lbs. of coal per mile, and evaporated one gallon per minute.

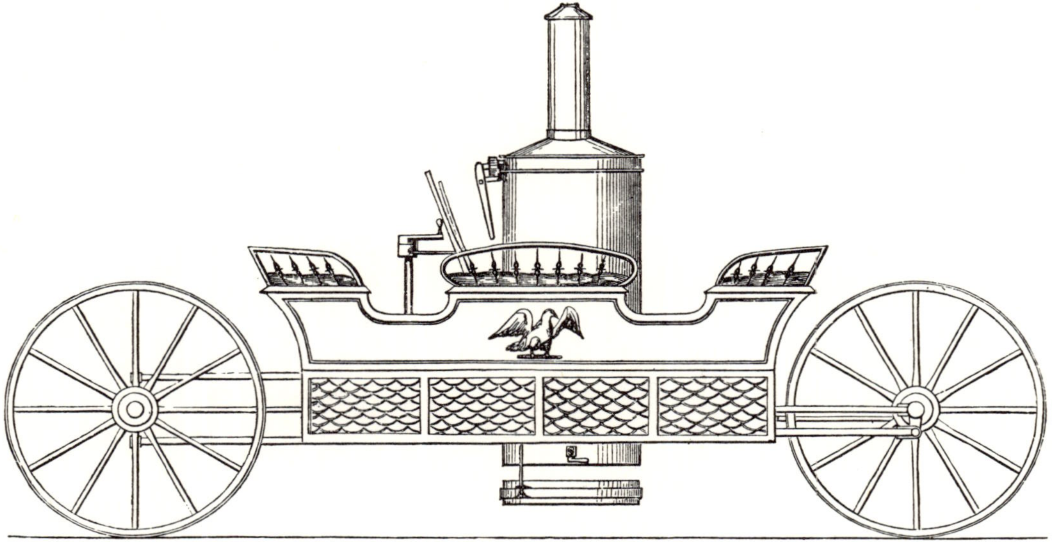

FIG. 12.—Fisher's Steam Pleasure Wagon (American), 1859.

[Mr. J. K. Fisher was one of the first Americans to pay much attention to the subject of steam road traffic. In 1840 he made a small steam carriage, and another in 1853, in which the boiler was composed of fourteen water tubes, each $2\frac{3}{4}$ inches in diameter, set around the fire, and provided with a steam chamber at the top, and a water chamber at the bottom; it ran at fifteen miles an hour on good roads. In 1858 Mr. Fisher made two self-propelling steam fire-engines, and in 1859 the steam pleasure wagon illustrated above. It made a few trial trips; its weight, with eleven men on it, was a little over five tons. On a gravel road with rather loose surface it did a mile in 2 minutes 40 seconds.—TRANSLATOR.]

IV

THE AUTOMOBILE AS TRACTION ENGINE

WHEREAS at the present time the automobile as self-propeller (*i.e.* not used to drag other carriages) has not much prospect of being widely adopted for military purposes, used as a means of traction much greater importance must be attached to it. It was for this purpose (*i.e.* as traction engine) that the Frenchman Cugnot proposed, in 1769, to the French Minister of War the construction of a steam motor wagon, by utilising the invention of his countryman Papin.

The Steam Motor in Competition with other kinds of Motors.

It is only a question to which driving power to give the preference. Besides the various gas mixtures used in explosion motors, steam and the electric fluid have to be considered. Of late years for stationary small power engines steam-power has been almost entirely replaced by the gas engine, and that again by the oil motor. It looked at one time as if the oil motor would play an equally preponderating part as compared with steam for transport on roads without rails. But in the different heavy motor competitions which have taken place in France and England recently (Paris in August 1897 and October 1898; Liverpool in May 1898), the steam-engine proved to be a formidable competitor.

Use of Mechanical Traction in different Armies.

For the transport of artillery, oil motors working up to from 8 to 15 horse-power can be used, and were so employed (system Jourdan) in the 1896 manœuvres of the French 16th Army Corps. In 1898 oil motors were used in Austria for the transport of artillery in hilly country by the 17th and 18th Army Corps. In England, on the other hand, in the August 1898 manœuvres only steam road traction engines were employed. Lord Wolseley, the commander-in-chief, reports with reference to them that they rendered valuable service in supplementing horse traction in wagon transport in rear of the army, easily accomplishing the task set them of drawing four wagons each with a load of five tons on level roads.

The Steam Motor more suited for Heavy Traction than others.

For heavy loads requiring greatest traction power (over 15 horse-power) the oil motor appears at present to be not so suitable as the steam road engine or the electric motor. As the power of the oil-motor working on the gas explosion system cannot be graduated, the driving shaft of the engine must always work at high speed. The danger of heating of the axles and break down of the valve packing is therefore very great, and the engine requires careful attention.

Apparent Lighter Weight of the Oil Motor.

In the strife of opinions between the partisans of the oil motor and the steam engine, its lighter weight is claimed in favour of the former. That may be a consideration for traffic in a particular district where the condition of the roads is specially favourable. But for military purposes one must reckon with the minimum of result obtainable on bad and soft roads and steep gradients. The expansion space of the gas must then be increased; thus the weight of the whole of the mechanism of the oil motor must be heavier than that of a steam engine of the same power.

The Steam Road Locomotive successfully used in War.

Of the use of the steam road locomotive in war we have historical evidence. As early as 1854 in the Crimean war the English army employed steam traction engines, on the Boydell system, for transport of wagon loads from the magazines at Balaclava to the front, over tracts of country impassable for other vehicles.

The street locomotive was used also both in the Franco-German war of 1870 and the Russo-Turkish war of 1878, and the experience gained ought to teach us to appreciate this means of transport, which has since then been so greatly perfected.

The importance of reserves in enabling an army to accomplish its task is more and more recognised since wars with great masses of troops were undertaken. Their employment in the war against Russia in 1812 showed that success in war does not depend alone on victorious battles, but also on the fulfilment of the conditions under which an army exists by means of assured supply.

Inadequate Communications in 1870 between the German Armies and Germany.

In 1870 the keeping up of communications between the German army and its native land, and the magazines established on the military roads, required an unparalleled quantity of vehicles. And although this system of supply could be protected if necessary, it should not be forgotten that it was only possible, thanks to the favourable conditions of the operation in a rich, highly cultivated country.

Need of substitutes for Animal Traction in the Campaign in Bosnia in 1878.

The campaign of the army of occupation in Bosnia in 1878 affords an example of the size to which the train of wagons may attain in an uncultivated country with incomplete communications. Here was seen a repetition of the experiences gone through by the French army in 1812 in Russia: the supply columns required such a service of men and horses, and were so long on the way, that only from one- to two-thirds of the loads which started reached the magazines in Sarajevo. The horses drawing the supply trains sent from Banjaluka to Travnick consumed repeatedly the supplies of oats they were taking, and had to be supplied out of the Travnick magazines for the return journey.[1]

[1] *Vedette*, 1898, "Essay on Load Transport in War," by Colonel Victor Filschkert, of the Austrian army.

The war of 1870 showed strikingly how important railways are for bringing up not only troops but also supplies, and how disturbing all interruptions are (such as the blowing up of the Nanteuil Tunnel, of the Moselle Bridge at Fontenoy, 7½ miles south of Toul, and the Xertingy Viaduct.

In future Wars, use of Railways in an Enemy's Country only to be reckoned on at a late Period.

Such experiences teach us that in future an army compelled to retreat will not leave the railways so undisturbed as formerly. For this reason it is now recognised that in future from the moment of invading an enemy's territory by the main army the use of the railways will cease. The destruction of railway lines is prepared for in peace time with other means than formerly, and to such an extent that it will take the railway service troops now found in all armies a long time to repair or rebuild the lines, even if they attained the strength of brigades. But until the lines are repaired supplies of all kinds not obtainable by requisition in the country itself must be forwarded by employing every available means of road transport.

Break down of Animal Traction in the Campaign of 1812.

Animal traction, which formerly had to be relied on, has such great disadvantages, that the substitution of mechanical traction is most desirable. In 1812 Napoleon set great hopes on the employment of draught oxen for his supply train, and the oxen were to be eaten when they had done their work. But they were slow and soon exhausted. The horses, on the other hand, required too much fodder, and consumed supplies intended for formation of magazines. In addition to this, disease caused by the eating of green food made such inroads in the supply of horses, that cavalry regiments were compelled to give up their mounts to provide the indispensable teams for the guns.

Mechanical Traction as safeguard in case of Epidemics among Draught Animals.

The danger of outbreaks of epidemics should supply another reason for not placing too much reliance on draught animals; for instance, in 1871 infectious horse diseases (influenza and glanders) threatened to break out in the teams of the transport columns in rear of the armies, shortly before the end of the war.

That, in spite of the well-known disadvantages of animal traction, mechanical traction is not looked on with much favour in the army is only justified when the use of motor vehicles with the columns of troops in action at the front is considered. Such use of them must be limited, as in this case the vehicles with the troops must, when the latter are encamping, leave the roads free, and be parked together on one side, for which oil-motor vehicles are quite unfitted.

Cause of Dislike of Mechanical Traction in the Army.

But the conditions are different in the rear of the army, where the columns can march as in peace time, and therefore no marching off the roads into the open country is necessary. Here mechanical traction may be employed with great advantage.

For draught purposes the steam road locomotives used to a small extent in the war of 1870 proved their value.[1] At that time only two of Messrs. Fowler's traction engines were bought by the Prussian War Ministry, and brought on after the army by the German civil engineer Toepffer.

The work done by these engines was, according to the '*Recollections*' of General von der Goltz as follows:—

Particulars of the Work done by Traction Engines in the War of 1870.

1. Transport of supplies in 12 French military baggage wagons for 30 (English) miles, from Pont à Mousson to Commercy, carried out in 2½ days.

2. Transport of a railway locomotive and tender, round Toul, from Pont à Mousson to Commercy in 2½ days.

3. Journey of the engine on the line from Commercy to Nanteuil s/M.

4. Transport of 700 cwt. of ammunition with 4 gun carriages from Nanteuil to Villeneuve St. Georges and back in 3½ days.

[1] Supplement to the *Militär-Wochenblatt*, 1886. 'Recollections of the Franco-German War, 1870-71.' By Baron von der Goltz.

5. Transport of a railway engine and tender from Nanteuil to Trilport, to get it by road round an unrepaired railway tunnel at Nanteuil (which had been blown up), and the uncompleted bridge over the Marne at Trilport, in 1½ to 2 days.

6. Transport of 300 cwt. of ammunition with 80 cwt. of coal from Nanteuil to Villeneuve St. Georges in 3½ days.

7. Transport of 180 cwt. of ammunition and 80 cwt. of coal with one locomotive (the other was laid up for repairs) in 3½ days from Nanteuil to Corbeil.

8. Trial journey from Corbeil to Villacoublay and Versailles with load of oats, with a view to utilising the locomotives in the regular transport of ammunition.

Precarious Supply Arrangements for the Army before Paris.

It will be seen that the two traction engines rendered good service, and a dozen of them would have been of great advantage to the army round Paris in getting the heavy siege guns and ammunition on to the plateau de Villacoublay. As the Army Service Corps was compelled to make use of every available vehicle, the army corps before Paris had to provide their own transport to obtain their supplies by way of Villeneuve St. Georges from the chief depôt. But the means of transport consisted chiefly in the teams of the field artillery, whose mobility in case of a serious sortie on the part of the French was thereby weakened. Fortunately, at this period of the siege the enterprise of the besieged had been too much damped by the failures of the earlier sorties for this weakness to be dangerous. But any one who was present with the field artillery before Paris will remember how this transport work exhausted the horses, and how desirable it was that the troops should be spared this drain on their equipment.[1]

The most important service was the transport of a railway engine, as the Germans had some rolling stock of different

[1] Blume, *The Bombardment of Paris*, 1870-71.

Fig. 13.—Maxim Gun mounted on a Four-wheel Cycle.

Fig. 14.—Dietrich & Co.'s Automobile Freight Wagon. (*See page* 16.)

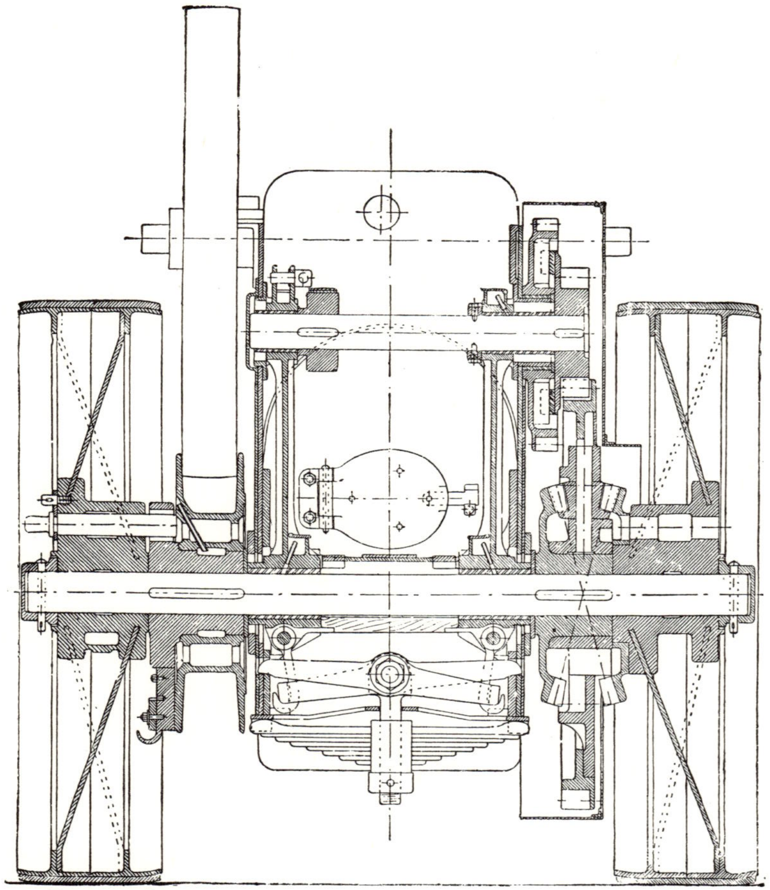

Fig. 15.—Section showing how Fowler Traction Engines rest on Springs. (Rear Axle.) *See page* 27.

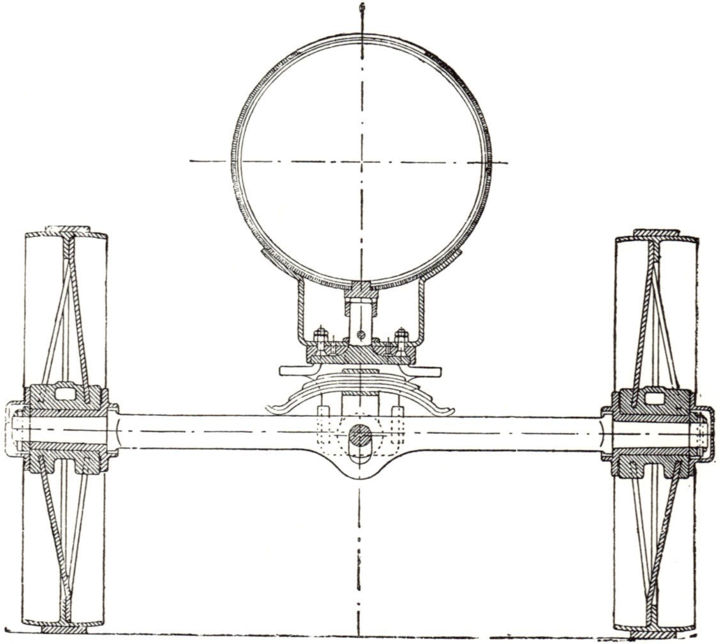

Fig. 16.—Section showing how Fowler Traction Engines rest on Springs. (Front Axle.)

kinds on part of the broken railway on the side next the enemy, but no locomotive. Transport of guns was rendered unnecessary by the conclusion of peace.

Results obtained with the two Traction Engines used by the Germans in the 1870 Campaign.

In judging the work done by the two traction engines used by the Germans in the campaign of 1870, it must be remembered that they were constructed as steam ploughing engines, and weighing twenty tons, were too heavy for passing over pontoon bridges. But even on short winter days and with bad roads a rate of fifteen miles a day was got out of them, and on longer days and better roads as much as twenty-five to thirty miles a day. Their rate of travelling was thus about the same as that of infantry on the march, which they could easily have kept up with.

In the Russo-Turkish war of 1878 both the Russian and Roumanian railways were badly provided with engines and trucks, and in the course of the campaign 120 engines and 2150 trucks had to be provided; also the railways were insufficient and over 200 miles of new lines were built in four months to provide for indispensable requirements. Thus there was plenty of room for utilising field lines and traction engines. Of the latter the Russian Government had purchased two in 1876,[1] which answered so well that ten new ones were ordered for the war and used during it, making twelve in all, of which two were made by Maltzeff, four by Clayton, and six by Aveling-Porter. According to the Report of Major Demianowitsch of the Russian army, these traction engines gave most satisfactory results, and effected very considerable saving of expense and labour.[2] Especially was this the case with the traction engines used by the Roumanian army before Plevna, which were also used in arming the batteries with guns.

[1] Bornecque, *Journal des Sciences Militaires*, 21st vol. 1878. 'Road Locomotives considered from a military point of view.'

[2] Russian *Invalide*, 24th February 1879, No. 42.

Interruption of the German Experiments with Road Traction Engines.

It is remarkable that, after being used in two great campaigns, so little was heard about preparations for their employment in war afterwards. In Germany this is to be explained by the fact that it is still a country rich in horses, and that therefore it is unnecessary to rely on the assistance of more or less complicated engines.

Extended Experiments with Traction Engines in Italy between 1875 and 1883.

But the conditions are different in Italy; here the supply of horses is scanty, and in case of war they have mostly to be purchased abroad. At mobilisation of the Italian army, a large part of it is obliged by the configuration of the country to make long marches up to the plains of the Po; and in order to get over this drawback, horse depôts were established in Upper Italy, and peace batteries were to be put on a war footing as regards teams only in this district, to which the guns, partly without teams, were to be brought by rail. But the railways were so congested with traffic that mobilisation of the army occupied (as compared with German conditions) the comparatively long time of from fourteen to twenty days. In order to relieve the congested state of the lines, it appeared to be most desirable to transport the guns and carriages without teams by means of road traction engines to the scene of the manœuvres, where the necessary teams would be provided from the horse depôts. With these objects in view, and under these conditions, during the period between 1875 and 1883 road traction engines were employed to a considerable extent. Engines made by Fowler, Aveling & Porter, and Enrico were purchased, which are said to have rendered good service, especially at the great manœuvres, when they drew guns and carriages over the Apennines. But the use of traction engines, so enthusiastically taken up by the army to begin with, was discontinued in 1883.

The engines were no longer so heavy as those used in 1870, their weight being only about ten tons, which the

Italian pontoon bridges were supposed to be equal to carrying. But the following disadvantages were advanced against them:—

Complaints against Traction Engines in Italy.

1. The engines required their boilers refilling every eight or nine miles, and to coal again every twenty-four miles (*i.e.* about 440 gallons of water and about half a ton of coal).

2. The engines could only draw about twice their own weight, and eight per cent. less on ascents.

3. There were continual breakdowns if the engines were driven fast, and to avoid this they had to be driven slowly, thus doing away with what had been hoped would prove a great advantage, viz. speedy transport.

4. Smoke and noise causing interruption of ordinary horse traffic, especially in narrow roads.

Special Wheel Construction for Protection against Shocks and Jolting.

Another disadvantage arose from the jolting, so much more severe on country roads than on rails. This ruined the engines, and quite exhausted the drivers standing on them. To overcome this defect special kinds of wheels were constructed with elastic material to cover them, such as full rubber tyres, also wooden wedges with some sort of buffer arrangement between them, over which the iron tyres were fixed.[1] But nowadays such complicated wheel construction is avoided by using springs, on which the axle-bearings rest (see figs. 15 and 16).

But the necessity for supplementing animal with mechanical traction is more and more experienced in Italy, the question being whether the steam traction engine or the oil motor carriage should be used.[2]

Although these experiments have not fulfilled all expectations as regards facilitating army mobilisation, it must be admitted that the traction engine alone has stood the test

[1] Major Mirandoli in *Rivista di artiglieria e genio*, 1875: also *Rivista militare*, 1876, vol. i.; 1878, vols. ii. and iii.; and 1883, vol. i.

[2] Luigi Segato, *Rivista militare*, 1898.

of military requirements—not so satisfactorily as might be wished, perhaps, but still it has stood the test, whereas such experiences with other automobiles are wanting.

Present Construction of the Road Locomotive.

The firm of John Fowler & Co., which supplied the road locomotives used by the German army in 1870, has improved the construction of the engines it makes for the English War Office and for industrial and agricultural purposes. They are now more lightly constructed, engines of ten tons weight working up to 50 indicated horse-power. Their construction secures better utilisation of the heating material, and therefore more economical working. The water-supply (60 to 90 gallons) only requires replenishing every eight or nine miles when working on a level road, and if a tender is used, of course at still less frequent intervals. The engines are provided with fire-boxes in which wood, naphtha, and agricultural refuse can be used as fuel.

Use of the Steam Road Engine as Stationary Power Engine.

A winding apparatus with drum (capstan) and 50 yards of steel wire rope is connected to the rear driving axle (see p. 54), by means of which heavy weights can be wound up steep places, or got out of difficult positions, the engine being firmly planted crosswise. According to the report of the Krupp Gruson-works, the Fowler steam road locomotive will draw after it a load of 22½ tons on roads with gradients of 1 in 12, and wind it up gradients of 1 in 8 by means of the drum and steel rope.

It will be seen that in this manner the traction engine may be employed in arming siege batteries. With it at night-time the heaviest guns can be got into positions far from the road much more quickly with the drum and rope on the fixed engine than by any other method. In employing horse traction for heavy loads on difficult ground it is well known that there is much waste of power, especially if teams of more than six horses must be used; and the use of large numbers of men at night is limited by the difficulty of getting them all to pull together and at the same time.

By means of a crane fixed on the traction engine the train trucks can be quickly unloaded, guns mounted on their carriages, etc., work which can otherwise be done only by tedious operations which delay the formation of the siege train as well as the arming of the batteries (see fig. 17).

Use of the Steam Road Engine and Crane combined.

The conditions which prevailed at the siege of Belfort in 1870 show clearly how useful in many ways would have been the assistance which mechanical traction could have afforded the foot artillery.

As the Bavarian siege-park at Rechotte was being formed on the 17th and 18th of December 1870, a 24-pounder fell over on the road. The artillerymen worked from five o'clock in the evening till half-past three in the morning, and in spite of assistance from horses of the field artillery, were unable to right it; and it was only by employing fifty men and eight horses in daylight that the attempt succeeded. For Battery 22, every 24-pounder had to be hauled up by ten horses and sixty men, and the same with Battery 52. For Battery 23, they were obliged to take the gun off its carriage and haul it on a sledge drawn by twelve horses and twenty-five men. To another gun one hundred and twenty men and eight horses were harnessed; after seventy metres it sank up to the hub, the ropes broke, and it took three and a half hours to get it out over planks.[1]

Delay in Transport of Guns when only Men and Horses are employed.

It was only on the 14th of September 1870 that the German artillery before Toul was able to get guns in place on the commanding position on Mont St. Michel. But the two Fowler road steam engines had reached Pont à Mousson on the 20th of the previous month. The driver, who was not then under military orders, rode from there to Toul to inquire if his engines could be employed. Seeing

Instance of how Traction Engines may be used to get Guns into Commanding Positions.

[1] Schlagintweit, *History of the 2nd Bavarian Foot Artillery Regiment.*

the artillery officers almost at their wits'-end as to how to get their heavy guns up the mountain, he offered to use his traction engines, which were fitted with windlass and steel rope, but his offer was declined.[1]

It is uncertain whether the few guns available could have been employed from this position with such effect that the early capture of the fortress might have been to some extent attributed to the use of mechanical traction. (The besieged had been encouraged by their successful repulse of a recent attack.) In any case, now that the service which the road locomotive can render is better known than it was then, it is worth noting that it can be employed with good results in similar circumstances.

[1] Report of Engineer Richard Toepffer of Magdeburg.

V

A MOTOR CAR WHICH CAN BE USED BOTH AS AUTOMOBILE AND FOR TRACTION

The Serpollet Steam Car.

OF recent years a new type of steam motor has come to the front, which differs considerably from steam engines of the Fowler type already mentioned. It was invented in 1877 by the French engineer, Serpollet,[1] and exhibited at the Paris Exhibition of 1878. In the recent (1894-1898) competitions between motor vehicles of all kinds, the Serpollet again attracted attention. In it the generator and motor are so small as to encroach but little on the carrying space or capacity.

Peculiar Construction of the Serpollet Motor.[2]

The generator consists of a spiral evaporator-tube, with slit shape bore of from 3-4 mm. diameter. In this extremely small bore evaporation takes place almost instantaneously, and the superheated steam at 250 to 300° C. enters directly under the piston end of the engine. The generator

[1] *Le génie civil A.*, xxxi., No. 7, p. 7.

[2] The first Serpollet instantaneous generator was made of strong copper tube flattened, so that the bore was almost closed up, and fitted in a spiral form over a coke stove in a cylindrical case. In the improved Serpollet, steel tubes are used instead of copper, and to increase their resistance the tube is made gutter shape and carried in rows in a rectangular case. To start the engine, water is pumped into the tube by hand, and when running, the pumping is done automatically. The tube is arranged in rows over the fire, that is to say, it is one long tube bent at intervals. The water enters at one end as water, and issues as steam at very high pressure at the other end. The peculiar shape of the tube will be understood if one takes a bit of quill or rubber tube, and presses one side of it in until it almost touches the other.—TRANSLATOR.

is tested under a pressure of 300 atmospheres, whereas in use only 25 to 30 atmospheres are required. This great margin of safety does away with any danger from explosion and the need of safety valves.

This motor was first used on a large scale for passenger traffic in Paris street omnibuses. The weight of the generator in this case is a little over half a ton; it is three feet high and long, and one and a half feet wide. The omnibus itself weighs nearly three tons; the generator, motor, water, and coal about one and a half tons, or four and a half tons without load, and about seven tons with forty passengers, to which must be added a car of nearly six tons, or a total weight of between thirteen and fourteen tons, moved by a motor, etc., of one and a half tons, or about nine times its own weight. The consumption of fuel is about two and a half pounds for the kilometre (1093 yards) per horse-power.

Special Advantages of the Serpollet Motor Car.

The special advantages claimed for this motor for the purposes for which it is at present used are: No danger of explosion, no smoke, no unpleasant smell, no great noise, small consumption of fuel, small requirement of water, easily controlled and guided, small cost of maintenance, ease of starting it and ascending gradients, and power of instantly stopping it. As the passenger car can be heated by the exhaust steam without extra cost, the price (15,000 to 30,000 francs, from £600 to £1200, according to outfit) is not excessive. In 1898 Serpollet steam cars were introduced for connecting the Würtemberg state railway with places within 14 to 15 kilometres of Stuttgart, which previously had to rely on the infrequent train service.

Drawback to Use for Military Purposes.

As regards the value of such steam wagons for military traction purposes there are no data to go upon. But there appears to be one serious objection which will not easily be overcome. For railway steam engines reservoirs of

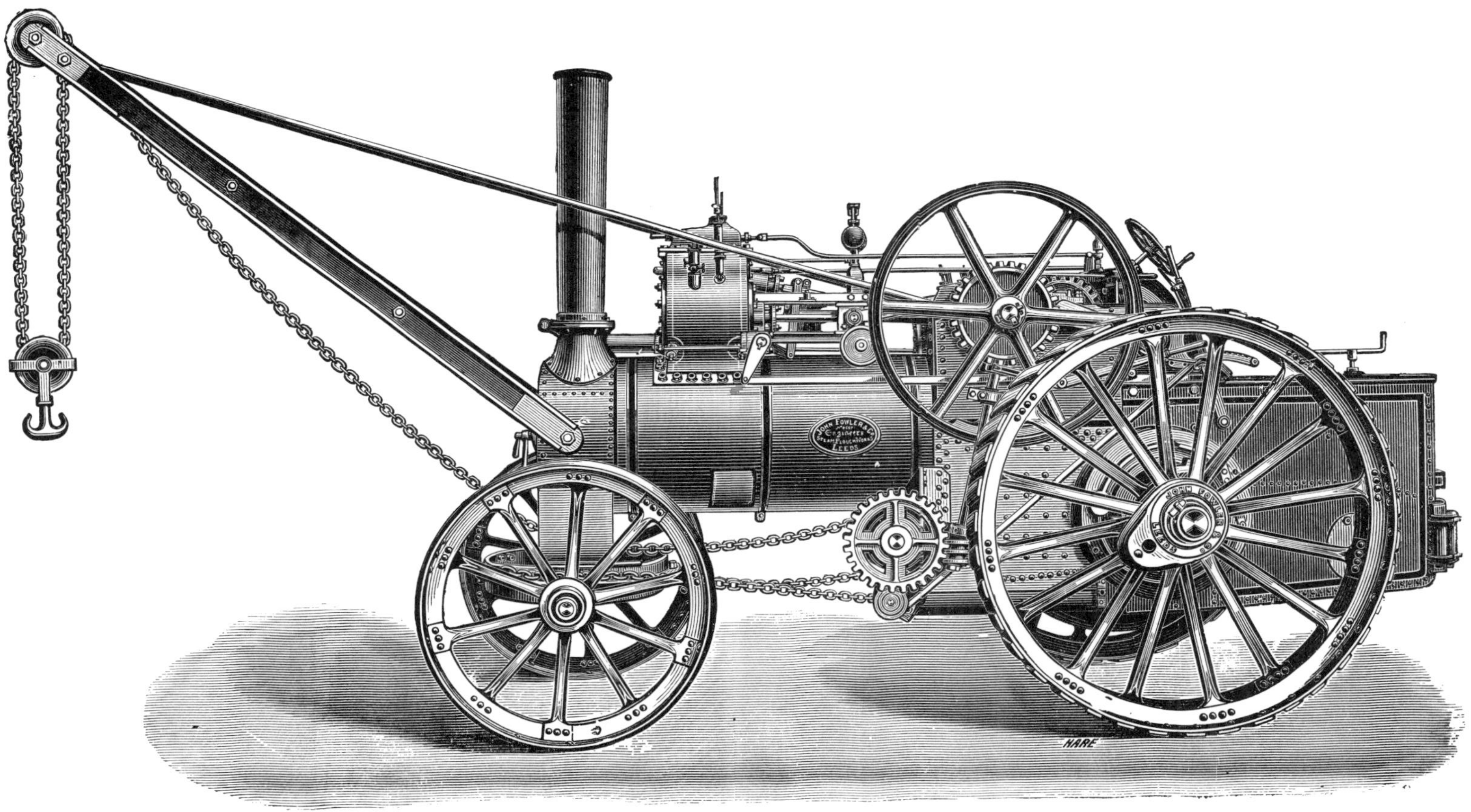

FIG. 17.—Fowler Road Traction Engine fitted with Crane. (*See page* 29.)

Fig. 18.—Serpollet Steam Motor and Cars.

Fig. 19.—The Liquid Fuel Engineering Company's Steam Wagon.

FIG. 22.—Fowler Road Traction Engine with Dynamo for supplying Electric Power and Light.

FIG. 20.—The Thornycroft Steam Wagon. (See page 32.

FIG. 21.—Train of ordinary Road Wagons drawn by a Fowler Traction Engine.

filtered, and where necessary artificially softened, water are provided at the stations. By their use, and with proper examination and attention, the formation of fur in the boilers can be so controlled as to reduce the chance of explosion to a minimum. With the traction engines hitherto used in war, of course any kind of water without regard to degrees of hardness had to be employed; but as the engines were not employed for long periods, not much inconvenience was experienced from this cause. The case is different, however, when it is a question of using tubes of such small diameter in the bore, and it is not easy to see how to guard against choking of the tubes caused by bad water taken often from dirty puddles.

Of what construction the steam motors were which were used in the English manœuvres is not mentioned in Lord Wolseley's Report.

Trial Races with Steam Wagons at Liverpool, 1898.

On the part of English makers and capitalists as great an amount of interest is being shown in the construction of steam automobiles as in France. This arises to some extent from the fact that at Liverpool in May 1898 a competition with automobile vehicles for heavy traffic took place, and as a minimum load of 2 tons was required, only steam motors took part in it. The conditions were very severe; and steam wagons weighing, loaded, from 5 to 9 tons developed speeds from nearly 6 to 12 kilometres (from $3\frac{2}{3}$ to $7\frac{1}{3}$ miles) per hour, taking gradients of 1 in 10 without stopping. But long stoppages were made by nearly all the engines in consequence of the tyres coming off wheels overweighted to the extent of 5 tons. In one of the engines a boiler tube burst.

Steam Road Engines or Steam Wagons.

At present, then, there are two kinds of steam motors available for road transport in war; the road locomotive (traction engine) and the steam wagon. The former is only for use for traction, but will draw whole trains of wagons, and therefore can be used for transport of heavy loads; the latter is primarily an automotor, and can be used only to a limited extent for traction purposes, such as for hauling single guns or a freight car. The idea of a train of vehicles on the road, each of them self-propelling and of a uniform light weight—calculated for the exigencies of roads and bridges—is doubtless attractive. There can be no want of traction power as long as fuel and water hold out, and full freedom in the formation of the transport column is assured. The comparatively heavy traction engine, on the other hand, will appear to many to be an unwieldy affair unsuited for military purposes by the side of the light and attractive steam carriage. Nevertheless, the military critic, bearing in mind the existing conditions of load transport, will give the preference to the traction engine, while admitting that for purely military requirements it is still open to improvement.

In the *Rivista di artiglieria e di genio* for December 1898, the Italian engineer, Major Mirandoli, writes strongly in favour of the traction engine, as will be seen from the following instructive remarks:—

Comparison between Transport Trains drawn by Traction Engines and other Automobiles.

Steam wagons using petroleum as fuel carry 1200 kilogrammes (23 cwt.) effective weight, the total weight of engine and load being 3000 kilogrammes (59 cwt.); so that ten such motors weigh 30 tons and carry a load of 12 tons. They require the services of twenty men, form a train of 180 metres (nearly 200 yards) in length, and cost 60,000 lire (=£2375). A train of wagons (composed of two-wheel wagons of Italian construction) drawn by one traction engine, drawing also 12 tons of load, weighs with its load 18 tons (without engine). With engine and two-wheel tender the total weight of the train is also 30 tons; but as compared with the steam wagon train, only four men are required, the length of the train is only 50 metres, and the cost is only 30,000 lire (=£1187). From this comparison it is perfectly clear that the advantage is on the side of the traction engine and train, especially as regards its shorter length of the column, as the train of automobiles with an average speed of 10 kilometres (about 6 miles) an hour necessitates a considerable interval between each motor forming the train, and of course the shorter the length of the train accompanying troops on the march in column the better. But for load transport BEHIND, *i.e.* in the rear of the troops, the advantage of mechanical traction consists less in shortening of the length of column, than in the fact that as compared with animal traction, the amount of work done in a day is more than double as much, viz. 70 kilometres (over 43 miles) at 10 kilometres (nearly 6¼ miles) per hour, as against 30 kilometres (about 18⅝ miles) at 4 kilometres (about 2½ miles) per hour.

The principal objection advanced formerly against the traction engine, viz. that the noise and smoke made horse traffic on the same road impossible, falls to the ground, now that in modern traction engines, such for instance as those constructed by Messrs. John Fowler & Co., the steam expansion is so utilised that the exhaust takes place at a pressure of only 0·4 atmospheres, almost noiselessly, so that in this respect the traction engine is on a par with the steam motor carriage.

At the Liverpool trial (May 1898) some of the steam wagons or cars used petroleum as fuel, and liquid fuel (petroleum, solar oil or German petroleum, naphtha, etc.) is used in place of coal for locomotives and marine engines. The English Shelline Shipping Company, for instance, which trades in petroleum from Batoum to India, uses petroleum as fuel in place of coal with advantage. In Southern Russia petroleum is also used on railways for fuel, and twenty-five railway engines are being built in England which will also only burn petroleum.[1]

[1] *Frankfurter Zeitung*, Handelsblatt 11th February 1899.

Among the advantages claimed for petroleum as fuel are:—

1. Greater heating power; twice as much as compared with coal.

2. Economy of space.

3. Simplified service; as the supply is automatic no stoker is required; and,

4. Ease of regulating the degree of heat to just what is required.

VI

ATTEMPTS TO REPLACE THE STEAM MOTOR BY OTHER KINDS OF MOTORS

Chief Defect of the Steam Engine.

NOTWITHSTANDING the fact that one of the objections raised against the steam locomotive is that the heat energy developed in its use is not fully utilised, it has until recently remained essentially the same as when constructed by Stephenson. But the invention of new motors and their competition with steam has caused improvements to be made in the steam engine with a view to adapt it for use both for small-power stationary and traction motors. Just as the incandescent gas light is the outcome of the fight for existence of the ordinary gas light against the electric light, so those interested in improving the steam engine have been spurred on by the results attained with gas engines and explosion motors.

A New Heat Motor in View.

Very recently yet another rival threatens the steam engine in the shape of the heat motor (*Wärmemotor*) invented by the Bavarian engineer Diesel, and first made generally known at the Munich Power and Engine Exhibition in 1898, though a great future had already been prophesied for it by engineering experts. Although at present in the trial stage, it is mentioned here because of the brilliant prospect which its use in connection with automobiles offers for military purposes.

Peculiarities of the Diesel Motor.

When the Diesel motor has proved suitable for stationary engines, its application for purposes of traffic will certainly follow. Like the explosion motors it works on the four-cycle principle, but with the difference that in this case neither electric nor incandescent tube or fuse ignition is used, but at the instant in which the fuel (coal dust or petroleum, etc.) is introduced into the working cylinder, it is ignited without explosion by coming into contact with the air in it, which has been heated to incandescence by the previous compression. In this connection it is specially noteworthy that in this new motor the energy developed out of the combustible material used is much greater than in other motors. Whereas in the best triple expansion steam engines it amounts to only 12 to 13 per cent., in the Diesel motor it is 30 per cent.

For military purposes the fact that the necessity for some special method of ignition is done away with is a great advantage. Electric ignition is quite unsuited for use in war on account of the difficulty of keeping the batteries and accumulators charged, and the incandescent tube is also unsuitable, being too liable to be affected by weather influences. Among other advantages claimed for the Diesel motor for military purposes, are:—

Advantages of the Diesel Motor for Military Purposes.

Absence of smoke and smell, which in other motors are said to frighten horses.

Small quantity of fuel required—240 to 250 grammes (120 to 125 oz.) of petroleum per horse-power per hour. This would allow greater distance between the depôts on the line of communications, and consequently it would be necessary to establish fewer of them. As no water for cooling the cylinders is required, as is the case in so many motors, the necessity for stoppages to get water and refill the cooling chambers is done away with.

Another great advantage is that the motor is always

ready to start work, whereas with oil motors it requires some minutes to heat them, and with the steam engine a quarter of an hour to get up steam. The starting of the Diesel motor is effected instantly by opening a valve in the supply chamber holding the reserve of compressed air (at 40 atmospheres), which at once starts the motor. The dependence of the motor on this method of starting it prevents its use at present for carriages; and especially for military purposes, as it would be risky to expose an apparatus containing gas at such high pressure to jolting on bad roads.

Advantages of Electric Motors for Traction Purposes.

Nowadays interest centres generally in the different applications of electricity. Many think of it first when it is a question of traction by mechanical means. As a matter of fact, both gas and steam motors have the disadvantage as compared with those driven by electricity, that the movement they communicate to the vehicle is by impact or shock. Whereas in the gas engine (benzine, etc., motors), which works with four-cycle cylinder, the explosion of the gas mixture causes a stroke of the piston at every other rotation of the driving shaft, in the steam engine, with every forward and return movement of the piston in the cylinder under the expansion of the steam, work is performed twice, *i.e.* with every revolution. In both the amount of power employed in driving the engine is different every moment, and in both dead points have to be passed, causing the movement to be jerky.

Advantages of Rotation Motors.

The ideal thing would be a power which would act perfectly evenly and regularly, and at every moment supply the same amount of driving power, so that no storage of live power in a flywheel would be necessary, and the transmitting of the rotation of the driving shaft to the axles of the running wheels be done either directly or by means of simple transmission.

Other Advantages of the Electro-motor for Military Purposes.

In the steam engine, and often also in gas motors, the attainment of this object is attempted by combining several working cylinders in which the stroke of the piston, exposed to the influence of the gas and steam, takes place alternately; thus the maximum effects of the pressure relieve one another alternately. But the electric motor is superior to all these arrangements in the regularity of its action on the driving wheels; it possesses also other very valuable advantages, which make it preferable to other motors when the electric fluid is obtainable. There is no fear of explosion, the steering is done by a simple hand grip, safety valves are not required, no great heat is developed, no smoke and no smell, and a motor of this kind can on occasion be driven at much higher power than its normal working power.

For driving vehicles with electricity accumulators are necessary—the Heilmann locomotive, in which the attempt is made to combine the use of steam and electricity (dynamo), not being at present practical.

Accumulators for Automobile Vehicles.

Accumulators have not made much headway for use for driving vehicles on ordinary roads. They are too heavy and too much dependent on arrangements for charging; also require too much care to be of use for military purposes. They are only suitable at present for use in and near towns with light vehicles which can run from 25 to 35 miles a day with one charging.

But it may safely be said that the time is not far distant when extended use will be made of light, dry accumulators which can be safely carried, and in that case means of recharging them will be as common as coal depôts are now. But, from a military point of view, of course, there can be no thought of sending accumulators back to their own stations to be recharged, and electric motor vehicles for war purposes can only be employed when the army is accompanied by power engines, like traction engines, which also carry dynamos (see fig. 22).

Put shortly, the present position of the motor question as regards the army is as follows:—Some of them are capable of development, but at present are incomplete, others are from the very nature of their construction too complicated at present to be thought of seriously for war purposes. The road traction engine, on the other hand, promises, with the recent improvements which have been effected in it, to prove of great value.

The Traction Engine superior to other Automobiles, as it can be used in so many different Ways.

The traction engine has the advantage over other motors of many-sided utility, and this point is a most important one in its favour. It transports in the rear of the army material of the most varied kind, at the railway termini it serves for unloading wagons, in camps intended to be used for some time it furnishes electric light, and does all the pumping necessary for supplying the water-tanks. Thus the army would possess in the traction engine a transportable power engine capable of being used in a variety of ways, whereas in the case of oil motors their use is confined exclusively to carrying loads and persons, and when not required for this purpose they are useless.

Transport of Preserved Meat in place of Cattle for Slaughter.

Of late renewed impetus has been given to the movement for using mechanical traction in the army. Mention has already been made of the difficulties connected with the supply of the enormous armies of modern times, even in the case of campaigns conducted in rich countries where supplies can be requisitioned freely. In such cases the 'perfected conserves,' or preserved foods, invented by Professor Emmerich of the University of Munich, combined with the use of mechanical traction in the army, enable it to dispense entirely with supplies of live cattle for slaughter; thus it can carry larger supplies, including other war material, more rapidly and for longer distances than formerly. This means greater freedom in operating for the troops in the fighting line, since supplies can be sent to them quickly from depôts at greater distances than formerly.

Facilities for the Formation of Supply Magazines.

Another important advantage offered by the traction engine is that when attached to the army supply corps they enable the latter to bring in supplies from a more extended district than that actually occupied by the army. As already mentioned, in such cases horse traction is unsatisfactory, as their day's march is too short, they consume too much of the supplies, and are subject to outbreaks of epidemic disease; in addition to this, the requisitioning of horses and carts in a country in which everything it required has already been requisitioned by the army on its march, presents great difficulties, and to get teams and carts from home means great delay. The traction engines of obsolete construction used by the German army in 1870 proved that steep ascents, bad roads, and narrow streets presented no insurmountable difficulties.

Even the very imperfect Traction Engine of 1870 got through when other Vehicles turned back.

An accident which may have had some effect in creating prejudice against the traction engine took place at the village of Maupertius, near Coulommiers, when the brake of a transport train with a load of 700 cwt. gave way, the engine being unable to hold such a weight on a paved street on an incline of 1 in 10. But according to reports of eyewitnesses the cause of the accident was defective construction in the vehicles requisitioned; in any case no one was hurt and but little delay caused.

Coal and Wood as easily obtainable in War Time as Oats and Hay.

The road traction engine requires coal as fuel, but can use wood if necessary, things not required by the troops on march, and which therefore may be requisitioned, or without great difficulty supplied from home, as they keep indefinitely in store, *i.e.* are not like perishable stores. It is therefore to the interest of the army to obtain in peace time as large a number of traction engines and trucks (fig. 23) as possible, and to arrange for a proper staff of trained drivers. To do this it is necessary that such means should be regularly employed for army transport in peace time. Other advantages would then be apparent, including economy of work and expense.

How to form a Staff of Trained Drivers for Traction Engines.

Calculations as to the comparative cost of horse and mechanical traction vary according to whether those who make them are prejudiced in favour of one or the other. But at present there is no basis for such comparison, as we do not know the extent of work, or the 'life,' of the improved modern traction engine, and so cannot get at its earning power and the percentage of return on the capital employed in it. But its durability is a very important factor; for instance, the two Fowler traction engines used, as already mentioned, in the war of 1870, have been in use ever since, and now, thirty years after, are employed as steam ploughs.

The Traction Engine Economical on account of its Durability.

For a regular daily traffic probably horse traction is cheapest, but if the traffic is occasional, as is the case in the army in peace time, horse service is not economical, *i.e.* if they are kept purposely; and if hired the expense is great, and there are other drawbacks. Under such conditions the traction engine can be employed with advantage, as it costs little when not in actual use, and yet permits the retention in service of a competent staff of men.

A special mechanical traction corps could thus be formed, in which, under proper officers, a staff would be trained for working steam and other automobiles for military purposes, and establishing repairing shops. It would be advisable to combine animal and mechanical traction, since both have to be employed either together or separately in forwarding supplies; at one time horses would be used, at another traction engines if available. For this reason this special corps would be attached to the artillery train

Formation of a Trained Traction Engine Corps.

rather than to the railway corps. The traction engine has only in appearance any relation to the engines of the railway supply corps. The Russian experiences are instructive as regards this point, since they showed that ordinary locksmiths managed the traction engines better than the drivers and firemen of railway engines. It is well known that there is so much difference between the ordinary railway engine and the field railway engine, that drivers of the former require a considerable time to learn how to drive the latter properly. Every type of engine has, as it were, an individuality of its own which the driver and fireman must thoroughly understand before they can work the engine economically and properly.

Other Advantages to be looked for from the Formation of a Traction Engine Park and Staff in Peace Time.

It is not to be expected that such a traction park would pay like a joint stock company. All the same it would be available for a variety of services for which otherwise vehicles would have to be hired; for example, in foraging and fatigue service, for which cast army horses are employed, which must be fed from the stores of horse forage required by the army generally.

For making earthworks in and around fortresses, transport of guns, etc., the traction engines, held in readiness for war, could be utilised. At manœuvres, the tactical handling of large bodies of troops could be carried out more independently of billeting, by the forwarding of the necessary bivouac supplies. Where it was necessary to make use of barracks, they could be established away from the large towns where land could be had more cheaply, and within easy distance of the drill ground.

In other special ways traction engines could be used in peace time: *e.g.* transport of heavy siege guns in foot artillery exercises, transport of the material of the balloon corps, for which they could also be used as power engines, either with or without dynamos; as engines for working and moving targets at field artillery firing practice in the country. At the permanent target practice grounds it is customary to use stationary engines to bring movable targets into range between the fixed ones, to represent all phases of a battle with artillery. With target practice in the open country, on the other hand, it has been necessary to employ horse power to draw the targets on sledges—a very unsatisfactory method. Apart from the fact that the artillery horses are used up and liable to get over-strained at this work, the resistance of the targets, especially against a wind, is so great that they must be very slightly constructed, or else moved very slowly.

VII

RELATION OF SUPPLY TRANSPORT BY MEANS OF TRACTION ENGINES TO THAT BY FIELD RAILWAYS

AGAINST the proposal to introduce road traction engines for use in war, it will naturally be suggested, 'But we have the field railway, on the metal rails of which ten times as much work can be done as is possible with the traction engine on ordinary roads—even under the most favourable conditions!'

It is necessary to repeat here what has already been said, viz. that a future war, entered on by two great states as a fight for existence, will be much more energetically carried out than formerly. And the population of the countries which may be the seat of war now know what is at stake. Many a Hotspur holds up as the ideal way of waging war that adopted by the Russians with such success in 1812. Though nowadays such drastic measures may possibly not be employed by civilised states, it will be necessary in future to be prepared at the outset of a campaign in an enemy's country for such a vigorous resistance as that which the French only began to adopt towards the end of the war of 1870-71 (by destroying railway bridges, lines, tunnels, as has been done in the present South African war).

The store of field railway material held ready in peace time will therefore barely suffice for completing and

Fig. 23.—Fowler Traction Engine with special Wagons built like Railway Trucks.

FIG. 24.—Fowler Road Engine on Rails. (*See page* 49.)

renewing the destroyed railways; such repairs may also take a long time to effect, and in the meantime road transport carried on by means of traction engines may be of the greatest value. This use of them alone ought to recommend them as worthy of being included among the war material, of which supplies are prepared beforehand in peace time.

Road Traction Engines useful as supplementing the Field Railway.

Supposing the supply of field railway material to be used up for repairing the railways, there is still the large amount required for siege operations to be remembered, which is not likely to be all procurable from home; and if it could, its transport from home to its destination would necessarily hinder the forwarding of other equally important war material.

Campaigning in an enemy's country means always some reliance on finding local means of transport, which is promptly requisitioned. In addition to horses, carts, wagons, etc., nowadays it is probable that the invader will be able to requisition the field railway (*i.e.* light railways, tram lines, etc.) now so commonly used for agricultural, mining, and other industrial purposes, that one may rely on finding it everywhere, except within a day or two's march of a fortress, whose garrison will have brought it into safety.

Road Traction Engines collect Field Railway Material before Fortresses.

For collecting a supply of such material (rails, etc.) where the engineer or the artillerist requires it for his siege operations before a fortress, the traction engine may be employed with advantage. The demand for horses, especially at every halt in the forward march of an army, is so enormous for the establishment of magazines of food and forage as well as the transport of guns, ammunition, etc., that not a horse will be available for transport of field railway material.[1]

[1] Kastenholz, *Die Belagerung von Belfort*, 1870-71: Berlin, 1875, pt. ii. p. 88.

The part which will be played by the field railway in future siege operations is clearly indicated by the following extracts from an essay on the subject by Major Tschilkert of the Austrian army:—'The field railway has a gauge of only 1 metre, its iron truck will carry guns of 6 tons weight (15 cm. cannon and 21 cm. mortars), two strong horses will draw it, even up gradients of 1 in 10 metres, strong stays (brakes) prevent it running back, and curves of 5 metre radius allow of rapid switching off into the battery positions; with the help of a special slide mount, the heaviest siege guns can be got on or off the truck, and moved on the rails over gradients of 1 in 10 metres to their platforms. With a railway of only 90 centimetres width laid in the trenches and covered ways and worked by manual labour, supplies of ammunition, etc., can be rapidly got up and distributed under cover night and day.'

Major Tschilkert adds: 'Future siege operations will know no difficulties in gun transport. The field railway transforms the whole terrain before a fortress into an easily-crossed communication space (*leicht überschreitbaren Kommunikationsfläche*). Roads before fortresses have lost their value.' But this brilliant future predicted for the use of rail tracks before fortresses, presupposes means for collecting and bringing up the railway materials scattered about the country (rails, chairs, sleepers, etc.), so that the traction engine employed in this work and the field railway are not only not competitors but allies—the work of one supplementing and completing that of the other.

It would rightly expose one to the charge of being prejudiced in favour of the road traction engine to assert that it could haul guns into position in the batteries without the aid of rails. That could only be done under specially favourable conditions—firm and not too uneven ground, with protected approach. The employment of the traction engine in such cases will be confined, as a rule, to well-made roads; away from these, and on soft ground, the engine could only be employed by being itself first driven over the ground, and then used as a fixed engine to wind up the load by means of the cable (see pp. 2, 28, and 94). The work in this case will be slow, but not so slow as when horses or men are employed.

Employment of Road Traction Engines in connection with Lines of Rails away from the Road.

The use of a metal rail-track in connection with cable haulage by the traction engine is almost imperative when the ground is very soft. In this case the line has the advantage of distributing the heavy weight over the sleepers, which for this purpose should be made broad. Further, the trucks or trollies can be so used that by coupling several under the load, the weight is distributed over a large number of wheels.

Conversion of the Road Traction Engine into a Railway Locomotive.

In combination with rails, the traction engine, used as a stationary hauling engine, with steel cable of 1000 yards length, if necessary, and rollers, can haul, or rather wind, guns over difficult and uneven ground, and up considerable gradients to high positions. For hauling loads on level ground it is also possible, in case of need, to run the traction engine itself on rails; and for this purpose they are now constructed so that the wheels can be changed, and those for use on rails adapted to fit the gauge of the particular line to be used. The material necessary for this purpose weighs about 1 cwt., and the time required in effecting the change is about two hours (see fig. 24).

It is unnecessary to insist on the importance of an army in an enemy's country being able to rely on its own engines in order to make use of the railways, as the opponent will take care not to leave his behind.

It is often possible to employ mixed transport by means

of road engines on the country roads, with a train on rails following it. But in this case, in order to avoid unloading, it is necessary that the vehicles for use on the road should be carried on the under-wagons or trollies (see figs. 25-27), of which, therefore, a supply should be kept ready in peace time.

Of late, in places where the local conditions are favourable, for instance, where waterfalls are available, electricity is taking the place of steam for use on field railways, and the well-known firm of Arthur Koppel, 96 Leadenhall Street, London, has worked out a system in which, by means of specially cleverly constructed electro-motor engines (see figs. 28 and 29), the conductors can be so quickly mounted, that the line can be constructed as rapidly as any other kind of field railway.[1] For military purposes there is no occasion to give the preference to electricity as motive power for field railways, as the mechanism required is too complicated, and the weight to be carried too heavy. But with the multiplicity of stations for supplying electric power for lighting and other purposes, there is no doubt electric power will be used for military purposes in war time when available.

Electric Field Railway in combination with the Road Traction Engine carrying a Dynamo.

For load transport on rails electric power offers many advantages, for military purposes, over cable traction, especially as the latter is often greatly limited as regards the length which can be used. But it is not to be expected that water-power engines or steam engines will be available just where the electric field-line is required for arming the batteries. In such cases the road traction engine could be used admirably as a dynamo carrier for supplying electricity. Several traction engines specially constructed and fitted could be used in such cases, either to deliver the electricity direct for driving power, or for charging accumu-

[1] *Zeitschrift für Elektrotechnik*, 13th February 1898.

lators. Naturally this entails the use of electric locomotives (fig. 15) for the lines.

Although the traction engine carrying a dynamo has hitherto been used almost exclusively for lighting purposes, it is possible to imagine conditions in which it would be desirable to use it for transmitting power.

VIII

MECHANICAL ROAD TRACTION MUST BE GENERAL IN A COUNTRY BEFORE IT CAN BE USEFULLY EMPLOYED IN WAR TIME

At present, as is attempted to be shown in this work, it is only proposed to use the steam road engine for replacing and supplementing animal traction in war time. But it is not to be supposed that the army will hold in readiness such a quantity of engines over and above what can be used in peace time as will be required in war; just as it only employs in peace time a fraction of the number of horses required for traction purposes in war time. It will be the same with the street locomotive and the benzine automobile. Their utilisation in war therefore depends on their being in general use in a country in peace time, as it is then easy for the military authorities, on the outbreak of war, to obtain all the engines necessary for meeting the most exacting of transport requirements.

The road locomotive has hitherto been used for the following purposes, viz.:—

1. For transport of heavy loads on country roads.
2. As self-propelling locomobile for steam ploughing and thrashing, etc.[1]

[1] More than thirty years ago, I remember as a boy seeing one of Messrs. Fowler's traction engines driving the machinery of a water flour mill, in dry seasons, when there was not enough water to keep the mill wheel going regularly. Only the other day, as I was reading the proofs of this book, I saw one of their engines, as cool as a cucumber, hauling three enormous wagons, with 30 or 40 tons of stone, up the steep, narrow, and crooked street near the New Inn at Pembridge, in Herefordshire—one of the oldest and

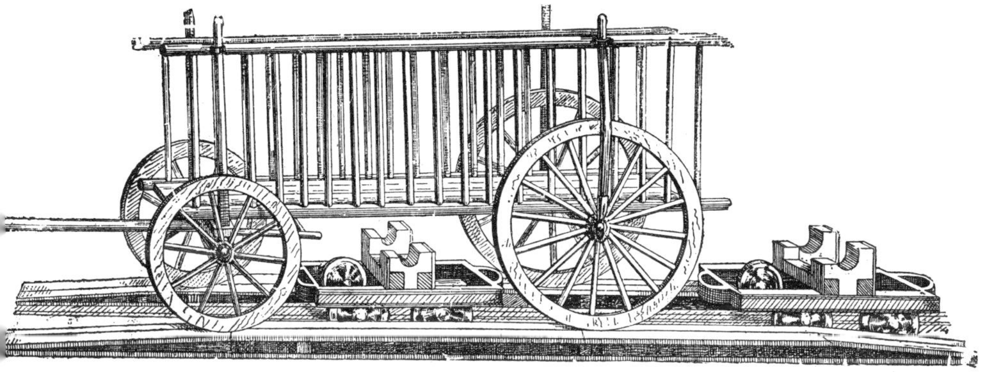

Fig. 27.—Wagon for use on Roads and also on Rails when mounted on the Trollies or under Trucks.

Fig. 25.—Wagon for use on Road and Rails.

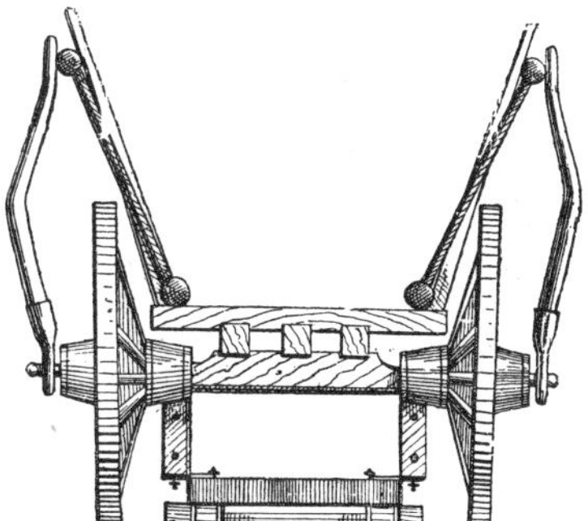

Fig. 26.—Wagon for use on Road and Rails.

Fig. 28.—Koppel's Wire Drum Truck for use with their Electro-Motor Engine (see Fig. 29). *See page* 50.

3. As steam road rollers.
4. As power engines for various purposes in the colonies.

Naturally engines constructed specially for steam ploughing and road rolling do not make such good road locomotives as engines specially constructed for road traction do. But just as the horse taken from farm work is not exactly the ideal animal for military traction, so in the case of war it will perforce be necessary in some cases to make use of engines not primarily intended for traction purposes, and adapt them to it as far as possible.

1. USE OF TRACTION ENGINES FOR TRANSPORT ON ROADS

The road traction engine is nowadays in very general use in England. Eight thousand of them were in use in Great Britain in 1894 for the transport of heavy loads on roads.[1] The weight of the loads which are turned out by the great iron and steel works (heavy guns and armour plates, etc.), is often so great that the railways are unable to deal with it. In such cases the only means of transport on land is on roads by means of traction engines—any damage done to roads or bridges being made good. In Germany the help of the traction engine is also called in in such cases.

The transport of minerals from mines to the railways

quaintest little towns in England. The stone was in lumps the size of a horse's head, and was for mending the roads. The traction engine deposits a load of these rocks at regular intervals along the road, and they are then broken into bits about the size of a hen's egg by *human beings* who sit on their coats on the heap and break the lumps with a hammer; they wear spectacles, and are often philosophers. But how curious for the steam engine and the stone age to meet in this way !—TRANSLATOR.

[1] *Journal of the Royal United Service Institution*, 1894, No. 198. Paper by Colonel Templer, 'Steam Transport on Roads.'

[As noted in the Introduction, the authorities were formerly the stumbling-block in the way of extended use of road engines in this country, but now that the roads have passed under the control of the county councils this restriction is removed, for the first thing a newly elected county council does is to buy a steam roller or traction engine.—TRANSLATOR.]

and works is often effected by means of traction engines. The field railway requires to be officially authorised in such cases, and this entails also getting consent from the commune or parish or district through which the road runs on which the line is to be laid. In many cases it would be necessary to make costly land purchases.

[A striking example of the value of the field railway is afforded by the great engineering undertaking now in progress for bringing water from the Welsh hills to Birmingham, the hundreds of thousands of enormous iron pipes being carried to their places on a light narrow gauge field railway.—TRANSLATOR.]

The road traction engine is also employed in England for purposes which would seem to have no sort of connection with war; for instance, in transport of circuses to country fairs, etc. And yet this particular use of it is of interest in judging of the value of the road engine for military purposes, because it gives a practical and valuable illustration of its many-sided utility. The traction engine draws the merry-go-round, taken to pieces and packed in wagons, from town to town, assists in putting up the staging, drives the machinery of the merry-go-round, and at night provides the electric light. The engine is thus in constant employment, and proves that it can bear such uninterrupted demands on its services without injury.

2. ITS USE IN DRAWING THE STEAM PLOUGH[1]

Use of the Road Locomotive in Steam Ploughing.

The road locomotive has almost entirely superseded horse power for transport of stationary engines for ploughing, etc., in England and elsewhere, after a long campaign between the advocates of the horse-drawn Howard engine and the self-driven Fowler engine.[2]

[1] For note on use of the steam plough in war, see pages 58*a* and 86.

[2] Cyth, *Wanderbuch eines Ingenieurs*, 1 and 2 vol. Appendix, 'History of the Development of the Steam Plough.'

For a long time past a system of ploughing introduced by Fowler, in which two road and winding locomotives are used, has also been most successful. In this case both engines are provided with horizontal, and in some cases vertical, winding drums, and draw the plough forwards and backwards across fields up to four hundred yards in width.[1] This system made hired ploughing possible in England and elsewhere, and proved specially useful for work on cotton and sugar plantations in tropical countries. In Southern Germany, where the land is divided up in such a way as to give but few opportunities for their profitable use on large connected estates, the costly double ploughing engines have as yet found but little employment. On the other hand, in Northern Germany there are already more than 500 Fowler steam ploughing machines on the double engine system in use—that is, over 1000 plough locomotives. Recently the same firm has met the demand for a steam plough suited for smaller and less expensive requirements, by reverting to the single steam road locomotive for the purpose. There is thus a prospect of more extended use of the steam plough in South Germany, where the agricultural community are coming to see that successful farming depends on utilising every possible means of improving the productive power of the soil. Not only does the steam plough do away with the tramping under hoof of the soil prepared for sowing, but the way in which the steam ploughshare turns up the earth, exposes a larger surface of it to the action of the air and thus increases the amount of chemical change of the soil so necessary for healthy plant growth. The capital outlay required for steam ploughs being beyond the means of most farmers, will doubtless encourage capitalists in South Germany to invest in steam ploughs in order to hire them out to farmers, as is already done on a large scale in North Germany.

Prospect of general employment of the Steam Plough in Germany.

[1] See Fig. 30 and Fig. 36.

3. THE STEAM ROAD ROLLER

Railroads increased the Importance of Ordinary Roads.

The introduction of mechanical traction is intimately connected with the question of road-making. Already at the beginning of the nineteenth century the road locomotive promised to supply the means of traffic on country roads, and was only prevented from doing so by the bad state of the roads. Then the railway secured the traffic by means of mechanical traction on rails. It became evident later that the country roads had not lost their importance through the railways. On the contrary, they were found, with the increased traffic, to be indispensable as means of access to the railways. Now, when the importance of the country road is universally acknowledged, improvement in its condition is also demanded. Much has been done in this direction, but much more remains to be done before it will be equal to the requirements of the improved means of communication and traffic offered by the various mechanical motors of the day;—in other words, the road has not kept pace with the roadster—at least, not with the mechanical one.

Better Roads demanded by the Advent of the Cyclist.

It is due to the cycle, which has become such an indispensable and universal means of transport, that demands are made, not only for improved and extended railway and canal communication, but also for better roads. This call for improved roads and streets is in its infancy; presently the owners of automobile vehicles will join forces with the cyclists, and finally it will dawn on the owners of carriages and other vehicles built for animal traction that good roads are good for their interests also, and that a rational method of road-making and maintaining must be introduced, one less trying to their carriages and cattle than the primitive arrangements of former times.

In this connection there is not so much occasion for the

laying down of new roads as in the improvement of existing ones, by making easier gradients, and where possible making detours round, instead of going straight over mountains as in the old obstinate way.[1] Then wooden bridges should be replaced by solid stone or iron ones.

Of prime importance is the proper treatment of the roads, so as to maintain them in good condition. The old system of 'mending' roads by covering the whole surface with broken stones to be ground down in time by the traffic is nearly obsolete, except in uncivilised districts.

At present there are two systems of road maintenance in use—the 'Flick' and the 'Deck' systems.

The Flick (= Patch) system consists in patching up the bad places in autumn and spring. The Deck (= Cover) system consists in spreading broken stone over the whole surface of the road as formerly, but with this important difference, viz. that instead of leaving it to be pressed into the bed of the road by the ordinary traffic, it is done by rolling.

For a long time this was attempted exclusively with horse rollers, but latterly recourse is usually had to the steam roller. Its advantages are considerable. Its pace can be regulated, and easily made twice that of the horse roller, which can only accomplish from 2 to 3 kilometres in an hour (say 2000 to 3000 yards). Interference with traffic is less. Whereas with the horse roller long stretches of road must be done at one time so as to avoid the expense of interruptions and utilise the hired horse power more economically, with the steam roller short stretches of 100 yards can be done, and are quickly ready for traffic again.[2]

[1] If there was nothing else left to judge them by, the character of the Romans for obstinacy and firmness of purpose would be evident from the remains of their roads, going as they do straight from point to point, over hill and dale and river, as though the road was made before the country it traverses was formed.—TRANSLATOR.

[2] Freiherr v. Rothenhan, *Die Entwickelung der Landstraszen.*

Moreover, the steam roller works not only better, but cheaper.[1] Since the road steam roller is widely used in peace time, its importance for use for mechanical traction in war time consists in the fact that by changing the rollers for wheels, it can be converted into a road locomotive.

Value of the Steam Road Roller for Military Purposes.

But in war time the steam roller will also be required, for repairing roads after the army has used it for marching. In view of the importance of country roads in the forwarding of supplies, it will be the duty of the staff intrusted with the forwarding of supplies to see that the roads are kept in good condition in this way.

4. ANOTHER SPHERE OF UTILITY FOR THE ROAD LOCOMOTIVE

exists in the colonies, which is indirectly to the advantage of the army, inasmuch as the greater the demand is, the more manufactories of them there will be, and the greater the number of engines which will be at the disposal of the army in war time. So long as official restraints handicapped their use, traction engines could make but little headway in England, and for a time the only market for them was in the colonies. In India and Australia before the introduction of railways the traction engine had to supply their place, and later to connect outlying districts with them. The traction engine is used to a considerable extent in Australia in wool transport. Fig. 35 shows, for example, an 8 horse-power Fowler compound traction engine which does a regular traffic in transporting about 8 tons of wool from Cowal Lake to Forbes, the nearest port on the Lachlan River. The day's journey across the open country, with no regular road, is 40 miles (60 kilometres). The same engine is employed at times in pumping water, ploughing, sowing, and for driving 16 Wolseley sheep-shearing machines.

[1] Franz Schumandl, *Die Mängel unserer Straszen und die Beseitigung derselben*, p. 20.

ADVENTURES OF A TRACTION ENGINE IN GERMAN SOUTH AFRICA

Pending the establishment of a railway, an attempt has been made to get over the transport difficulty in German South Africa by employing a traction engine obtained from England. The traffic with oxen was so difficult across the 60 miles of coast desert, in which the poor animals often got nothing to eat for a week, that they perished by hundreds, the whole way between Walfischbay and Swakopmund being white with their bones, and those which got through were mere skeletons, which required two months to get strength again.

The traction engine, from the time of its arrival at Walfischbay, where it was landed, until it reached Swakopmund, went through a series of adventures, which show under what peculiar conditions this method of transport has to be carried on there.

Difficulties of Traffic with Traction Engines in the Colonies.

Although the want of rain caused absence of that softness of the ground which is a hindrance in other colonies, working the engine through sand offered extraordinary although not insuperable difficulties. For ground of this nature the engine is provided with spuds, which are fixed to the driving wheels, and grip into the ground. The almost insuperable difficulty is the quantity of coal and water required in such arduous work, and the difficulty of getting it in the desert. The chief question of course is, Does it pay to use a traction engine under such conditions in the colonies? Lieutenant Troost, the owner of the engine, says it does, as with an outlay of 1640 marks for three journeys in a month there was an income of 1800 marks, or a 5°/₀ profit on the capital employed; but that this was only a theoretical estimate, the actual result being more favourable.[1]

Under what conditions the traction engine can be em-

[1] *Kolonialblatt*, January 15, 1899.

ployed in the other German colonies remains to be seen. Its proper place is as the forerunner of the railway, and when the materials for that are to hand, the traction engine does not wait the fate of being pushed on one side as useless, but rather does all kinds of useful work as a stationary engine, or works on the line as a locomotive after the necessary change of wheels.

Use of Benzine Automobiles in the Colonies.

In the French Soudan two automobile freight wagons have been at work this year, to keep up traffic connection during the eight rainless months of the year, between St. Louis and Kayes. The cars are built to carry 1200 to 1500 kg. (21 to 27 cwt.), and so far are said to have answered; and if the attempt succeeds, similar wagons are to be employed in traffic between Tamatave and Tananarivo in Madagascar. In this case the automobiles are intended to facilitate the formation of a railway, and then to be used for connecting the railway stations with the interior of the country. Between Makatsara and Tananarivo a service with automobiles is also projected, for which a special road is being constructed.[1]

Use of Traction Engines in the South African Campaign.

In November 1899 the English military authorities sent out 15 traction engines, mostly of Messrs. Fowler's make, for use in the South African campaign.[2] A special Traction Engine Corps has been formed under Major Templer (referred to in Section VIII. of this work), who has organised in peace time a special road locomotive service. Major Templer has also taken out a couple of 20 horse-power (nominal) Fowler steam ploughing engines, with deep-trenching ploughs. These ploughs, built on the same lines as those used in vine culture, and worked with a 400 metre cable, throw up a furrow 80 centimetres deep and 60 wide, which, with the earth taken out of the furrow, makes a pretty high breastwork. It is proposed to construct entrenchments on the lines of communication in this way.

[1] *Journal des Sciences Militaires*, August 1899. [2] See also pages 86-95.

FIG. 29.—The Koppel Field Railway Electro-Motor Car. (Electric Locomotive.) *See page* 50.

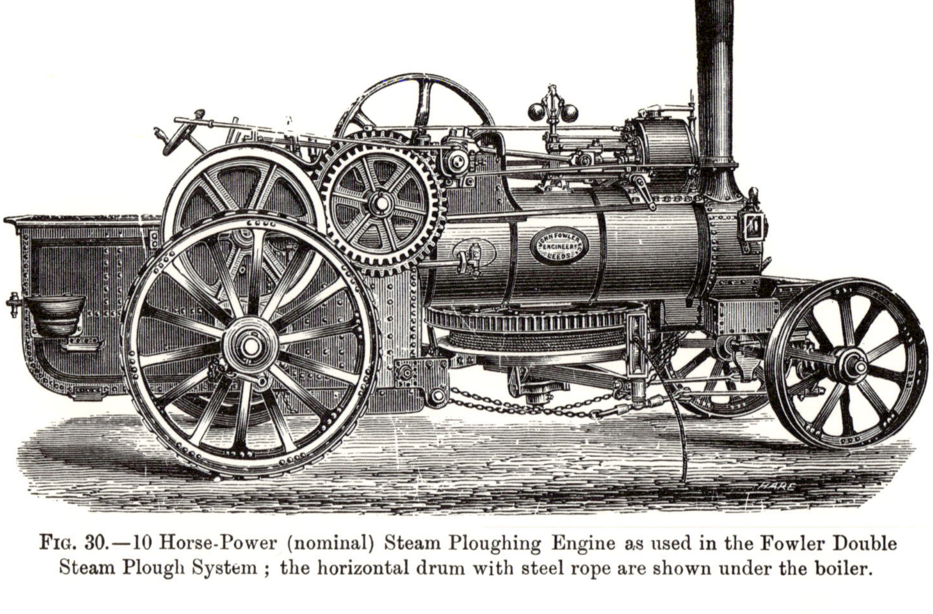

FIG. 30.—10 Horse-Power (nominal) Steam Ploughing Engine as used in the Fowler Double Steam Plough System ; the horizontal drum with steel rope are shown under the boiler.

FIG. 31.—The same Engine as Fig. 30 with the Drum removed, for use as Traction Engine.

APPENDIX

RÉSUMÉ OF EXPERIMENTS IN MECHANICAL TRACTION WITH ROAD LOCOMOTIVES FOR WAR PURPOSES[1]

French Experiments, 1875[2]

TOWARDS the end of 1875 experiments were made on the Champ de Mars at Paris with an 8 horse-power Aveling traction engine, which drew 12 field-guns and 6 empty and 1 loaded ammunition wagons. With this train, which was 124 metres (135 yards) in length and weighed 33 tons, various evolutions were satisfactorily carried out at a speed of 7½ kilometres per hour (4 to 5 miles). The French Government thereupon ordered some engines from Messrs. Aveling, but as a French engine of another type, which claimed certain advantages was offered, the French authorities could not decide which to have. The French engine developed 25 horse-power, but was about 6 tons heavier than the English engine.

Russian Experiments, 1876[3]

During the summer of 1876 experiments with road traction engines were made at the Krasznoje-Selo camp and near St. Petersburg.

[1] Previously published by the author in the October 1899 number of the *International Army and Navy Review.*

[2] Bornecque, *Journal des Sciences Militaires*, vol. 21, 1878. 'Les Locomotives Routières considérées au point de vue militaire.'

[3] Bornecque and Major Schulz, *Mittheilungen über Artillerie und Geniewesen*, 1877. 'Ueber Straszenlocomotiven.'

On July 25, 1876, a 9½-ton Aveling engine was driven over the road from Krasznoje-Selo to Ropscha, and was then put through various evolutions on the exercising ground, such as crossing a ploughed field and ditch, and descending a declivity of 1 in 6 metres to get water from the Dudergof Lake.

As a second experiment, on July 26, 1876, the engine was tried successfully on soft ground. The wheels sank 0·30 metre into the soft ground and the pace was reduced to 2½ kilometres per hour—but there were no stoppages. On the return journey a still worse and narrow country road was selected which sloped to one side. The ground was exceptionally slippery, the engine slipped continually but got along.

At a third trial the guns and ammunition wagons of a 9-pounder battery with the gunners were attached to the engine and various evolutions carried out. The train was so arranged that only the first three carriages were in line, each of the others being 1½ paces out of the track of the one in front of it. An attempt was made to take this train down a steep declivity—when the first gun, which had no brake on the wheel, threatened to fall over, but the engine was stopped in time. The engine was then detached, sent up a steep bank where it was fixed as a stationary engine, and by means of a wire cable hauled all the guns and train up at one time.

Messrs. Fowler had sent an engine to take part in the same trials, but it weighed 11 tons, which was found to be too heavy, especially for passing over the wooden bridges on the road between Kolpina and Uft-Ischora. As the driver of the Fowler engine would not wait until the bridges had been strengthened, he had the banks of the stream levelled a little and then drove his engine through the stream. This was considered a great triumph for the traction engine, as at the place where it crossed the stream was impassable for ordinary vehicles.

Then at the manœuvres extended experiments were made—some of them in the presence of the Czar—in the transport of heavy guns. In this case the engines were driven over uneven ground and thorn-bushes from the engineer park up to the first parallels to fetch the siege guns out of the batteries. In the same way Messrs. Aveling's engine brought 40-pounders right into the batteries, the Fowler engines working under the same conditions chiefly as stationary engines with the cable.

Later on at St. Petersburg experiments with fuel were carried out, which showed that with an Aveling engine two stears of wood as fuel sufficed to drive it for two hours (stear = cubic metre).

On the 13th of August, at St. Petersburg, in experiments in transporting baggage, 10 wagons with a gross weight of 34 tons were taken 26 kilometres (16 miles) in 5 hours and 25 minutes.

There was no considerable difference in the results obtained with the Aveling and Fowler engines; the former being lighter were preferred.

The results showed :—

(1) The power of guiding the engine is very great, as it can turn in a road nine paces in width.

(2) Drawing a load up to 4 or 5 tons a rate of 7½ kilometres can be maintained, with a consumption of fuel supply in the tender in 2½ hours.

(3) On good roads the engines can draw five times their own weight; with half this weight a speed of 4 to 6 kilometres per hour can be maintained.

(4) On bad country roads the load must not exceed 1½ times the weight of the engine.

(5) The engines can take any gradients which ordinary horse wagons can.

(6) The road traction engine can be very successfully used as stationary engines.

Employment of Road Traction Engines in the Russo-Turkish War, 1877-78[1]

In addition to the Aveling-Porter and Fowler traction engines used in 1876, others were used during the winter of 1876-77, so that the Russian army had then a dozen of them at its disposal, together with a quantity of wagons specially constructed for use with traction engines.

In order to train a staff of drivers and stokers, 54 men of the Railway Brigade were told off for this service. At first instruction was given by men sent out by the English firms; afterwards this was done by Russian officers, with the aid of a manual in the Russian language.

As early as the spring of 1877 it was manifest that the Russian soldiers trained as traction engine drivers were in every way as capable as the English drivers.

With the aid of two field smithies a repairing shop was formed, with three locksmiths to each smithy.

A staff officer and lieutenant had charge of the traction engines, and accompanied them on horseback when at work.

On April 19, 1877, by imperial command, the engines with their wagons and the two field smithies were attached to the army, and were employed at Fort Venderels for transport of siege material.

After a few trial essays, the engines began work by bringing guns and other artillery material up to the railway, on which they were then to be forwarded. In this way between the 7th and the 25th of May 1877 21,500 pud (430 German tons[2]) were carried from 2 to 12 kilometres.

On the 19th, 28th, and 29th of May 1877 the traction engines

[1] Report of Major Victor Demianovitsch of the Russian General Staff (Transport Department) on the work done by road traction engines during the Russo-Turkish War.—*Russian Invalide*, February 24, 1879.

[2] The German tonne weighs rather less than the English ton, viz. about 2205 lbs. as against 2240 lbs.—TRANSLATOR.

were sent, together with the artillery material, to the Danube, viz. three engines to the station at Baniassi, and nine to the town of Slatina. At Baniassi there was nothing for the engines to do. At Slatina four were used in transporting artillery material from the railway station along the country road to the military park 3 kilometres distant (nearly 2 miles). The guns and other artillery material thus carried weighed together over 200 tons.

After the guns had been got into position in the batteries there was no further work for the engines, and they were hurriedly sent off to Tourn-Margoorelli, nearly 70 miles away, about 40 of it being on a high road (*chaussée*), and about 30 on a country road or parish road (*vicinalstrasse*), where they arrived on June 13, 1877.

At Tourn-Margoorelli, although the weather was fine and the roads good, the engines were not used, the work of arming the batteries being done secretly at night; this accomplished, one engine was employed in placing electrical apparatus and in alterations in the siege park arrangements.

After the passage of the Danube, on the 19th June 1877, the road traction engines were again hastily sent off to transport a stationary engine with electrical apparatus to the town of Simnitza, about 28 miles distant. Again at Simnitza, from June 26 to August 12, in spite of fine weather and good roads, no work was found for the traction engines. On August 12 they were ordered by the commander of the siege artillery to Parapan, 30 miles away, to do transport work between that place and Petroschani, about 8 miles of country road. In this way about 520 tons were carried between August 15 and September 15.

When this work at Parapan was finished, as the bad time of year was approaching, all the engines were collected on September 18 at the Frateschti railway station, where on the highroad between Bucharest and Giurgevo they could be employed even in bad weather. Notwithstanding this they were not worked between September 18, 1877 and March 28, 1878, when, by special order of the Grand Duke Alexis Alexandrovitch, they were employed in transporting a steamer and 124 tons of coal from Giurgevo to Petroschani (about 22 miles) on the country road. The engines were then laid up, only one of them being employed at Frateschti railway station in pumping water, which work it executed from October 30, 1877 to July 1, 1878.

It was not until the spring of 1878 that work was again found for the engines, viz.:—

(1) Transport of siege material from the Banias station to Giurgevo, 14 miles, 9 of them being on the high-road, and 6 on ordinary country roads. At Frateschti there was an intermediate station for coaling and watering, and for minor repairs.

(2) Transport of siege material from the Slabodlia batteries (Nos. 1, 2, 3, 7, 8, and 10), in the Slabodlia Valley, to Port Saint-Nicolas, and to the town of Giurgevo, at distances of from about 3 to 7 miles.

(3) Transport of ammunition from Petroschani to the station of the same name, 1 kilometre distant, on the country road.

From the 23rd March 1877 to the 27th June 1878, about 5000 tons of material of different kinds were transported, in addition to the work done in pumping, by one engine, as noted above.

After completing this work on the left bank of the Danube, the traction engines were sent on rafts to Rustchuk, where they were to transport artillery ammunition from the harbour to the siege park, about 2½ miles distant; they were also employed in transporting guns, ammunition, etc., being sent back to Russia, from the park to the harbour.

In this manner 4000 tons were forwarded between July 2 and October 11, 1878, in addition to 800 tons of field guns from distances of from 2½ to 4 miles.

Although, on account of want of work for them, the traction

FIG. 32.—Fowler's Traction Engine which can be converted into a Steam Roller (see Fig. 17).

Fig. 33.—Fowler's Traction Engine (see fig. 32) used as a Steam Road Roller.

Fig. 34.—Fowler's Deep-Trenching Plough. (Cuts a furrow 30 inches deep and wide.) *See page* 86.

engines were unemployed half the time, according to the official report they transported for the army in the field 9141 tons of different material between April 28, 1877 and November 19, 1878.

In order to get a correct idea of the work done by the traction engines, it must be remembered that the contract price for animal transport for 1 pud (about 36 lbs.) from Simnitza to Giurgevo and to Parapan and Petroschani cost from 40 to 50 centimes. At this rate the transport work done by the tractions would have cost 69,758 roubles (over £11,000). If to this is added the cost of transporting the steamboat and the pumping work, the total cost, if done by animal traction, would have been 72,794 silver roubles, or at the then rate of exchange, 116,471 paper roubles.

In comparison with this, the capital expenditure and working expense of the 12 engines, including maintenance up to January 1, 1879, cost :—

	Roubles.	Copecks.
For 12 engines with interchangeable parts and 12 wagons, . . .	79,973	38
Two field forges, ...	3,660	20
Salary of instructors, ...	900	
Taking to pieces, etc. (*Zerlegung*), . .	731	1
Pay and maintenance from April 8, 1877 to April 5, 1878, ...	11,820	
Pay, etc., from April 8, 1878 to January 1, 1879, ...	8,595	
Dismantling, etc., ...	1,522	4
Coal, grease, etc., ...	7,315	83
	109,517	46

Thus it will be seen that although the engines were not all used, and only worked about half the time, they not only covered their original cost and working expenses, but saved 6954 roubles 14 copecks (over £1100) as well.

The engines were very serviceable and easily controlled. They might have rendered great service in the siege operations. As they were provided with cranes lifting 6 tons, it would have been easy with their help to have mounted the guns in the batteries, and loaded and unloaded heavy goods for the railway traffic, etc.

The traction engines have the additional advantage of being easily converted into locomotives for use on rails by changing the wheels. They were provided with steam pumping apparatus, so that water could be taken direct from streams or springs, thus avoiding tedious water carriage for them or hand pumping.

The loads were carried in special wagons or ordinary freight wagons, to which the engines were attached. Often as many as eighteen were in one train. The coupling of the wagons by means of iron clips (Demianovitch system) answered well, and can also be used for guns. A single engine is able to draw an entire field battery.

An important experience gained was (as confirmed also by English experiments), that ordinary locksmiths made the best drivers, as railway engine drivers, in spite of strict orders, would drive the engines too fast, which soon used them up.

The war services of traction engines have answered the expectations anticipated from the 1876 trials, and may be summed up as follows:—

1. The road traction engine can be usefully employed in transport on high-roads as well as on byroads. But to work in soft and sandy ground, the driving wheels must be altered and the whole weight of the engine reduced.

2. The turning power of the engine is excellent, as it only requires a width of road equal to double the length of the engine.

3. With reduced loads, viz. from 6 to 8 tons, the engine can travel at the rate of 6 to 7 kilometres (3½ to 4½ miles) per hour. If a tender is employed, the water-supply will last for 2½ hours.

4. On high-roads, or well-kept byroads, a single engine will

easily draw 50 tons, or five times its own weight, at 3 to 4 miles an hour.

Experiments in Italy, 1873-1883[1]

The first engine was procured in 1873; in 1874 the army was using ten, and in 1876, sixty. These engines were supplied by various English firms and also by one Italian firm (Enrico). No official report of the results of the experiments has been published, and the only information obtainable is from articles, contributed to the military journals by some Italian officers, on the construction and use of the road traction engine.

The first engine employed (1873) was one of Messrs. Aveling and Porter's, which was tested at Verona by the 8th Field Artillery regiment. In June it was reported of this engine that it would draw eight to ten wagons, with a load of 15 to 20 tons, 18 to 25 miles a day.

Other experiments took place at the camp at Castiglione delle Stiviere, where a regular service for the transport of hospital wagons was arranged, doing a daily journey of 12 miles with six to eleven wagons.

Further experiments on the ordinary roads between Verona and Turin proved so satisfactory that ten traction engines were ordered, varying from 4 to 12 horse-power. The weight of the engines was 1 ton per horse-power, and they drew three times their own weight up to a 5 per cent. gradient, twice their own weight up to 7 or 8 per cent. gradient, and a weight equal to their own up gradients of from 10 to 11 per cent.

The consumption of wood amounted to 2 lbs., of coal 1 lb., for each ton of the total weight.

For a ten hours' journey, *i.e.* 25 to 30 miles, the cost for oil etc., was 3 francs.

[1] Stella Sabino, 'Locomotive Stradali,' *Rivista Militare Italiana*, April 1876; and Mirandoli, 'Le Locomotive Stradali,' *Rivista Militare Italiana*, January and February 1883.

When necessary the winding gear can be used.

The average pace on good roads is 3 to 4 miles, on bad roads $1\frac{1}{2}$ to $2\frac{1}{2}$ miles, with a train up to 60 or 65 yards in length.

One important fact resulting from the experiments was that the weight of the train should not exceed two-thirds of the maximum weight which the engine can draw, in order to avoid having to take the train over bad places in sections, and to economise fuel and not overstrain the engine.

From the articles referred to it appears that the question of wheel construction was for a long time under consideration. The rubber covered wheels (Thompson system) offered certain advantages, but were abandoned as too complicated, and in the warm climate of Italy it is to be feared that rubber will not preserve its elasticity for more than a year. Attempts to protect the rubber from external influences led to expensive and complicated construction.

A noteworthy bit of work done by a traction engine was the transport of a 32-centimetre (=12·599 inch) gun from Turin to the camp at St. Maurizio. In this case a weight of 50 tons was carried on four wheels (gun 37, carriage 13 tons).

At Spezzia 24-centimetre (=9·449 inch) guns were moved into the batteries with the traction engine, as it was impossible with animal traction. The work was easily done and at less expense.

As regards the training of the drivers, it appears that:—

Eight or ten days' daily instruction was sufficient to train an intelligent soldier to drive an engine under ordinary conditions, and a month for extraordinary ones. But as the engine-driver must also be able to effect repairs on his engine, two years' training are required, and it is desirable that he should be a skilled mechanic.

As compared with the railway engine, in the traction engine the water level and temperature change much more rapidly, and the shocks to which the engine is exposed are much more violent.

The driver must thus be careful, clever, and intelligent. With care, in good hands, an engine will run for from four to six years without requiring very much repair, and may be serviceable for fifteen or twenty years before becoming 'old iron.'

In 1883 the use of the traction engine for military purposes in Italy was abandoned. The engines had not arrived at their present perfection of development. Captain Mirandoli of the Italian Engineer Corps refers to the Fowler engine as the best and steadiest for use on ordinary roads for medium and slow work.

Experiments in Switzerland in 1892[1]

A traction engine was employed at Andermatt in August 1892 in the heavy gun exercises, both for drawing and lifting purposes. Fitted with the crane apparatus, it was used for unloading material (mortars, etc.) brought up by the military line to Göschenen. It was proved that the engine can do good work in unloading, and probably better still in loading trucks, though some previous practice in attaching the loads to the crane and working the engine in this way was necessary, and the rails should not stand too high off the road so that the crane can work just at the right height. The engine was then driven from Göschenen to Andermatt, the $2\frac{1}{2}$ miles being done in $1\frac{3}{4}$ hours, including stoppages for water and to allow other vehicles to pass. The average pace uphill was about $1\frac{1}{4}$ miles per hour, the engine drawing a wagon containing the dismounted crane apparatus.

The journey from Andermatt to Baezberg and back was then accomplished without difficulty, but without wagon, and the engine had to pass a gradient of 17 per cent. on a very stony road. At the artillery park, by means of the crane, two 12-centimetre (4·742 inch) guns were lifted from the trunnion holes and laid in the marching rests. The engine was also used in transporting two 12-centimetre (4·742 inch)

[1] Report of Captain Stuerler of the Swiss army.

guns with their carriages to the military station on the Grossboden. Some difficulty was experienced in consequence of the soft, damp nature of the ground round the artillery park, but this was got over by sending the engine first over the bad parts and then using its drum and cable arrangement for winding the guns, etc., over after it.

On the Oberalpstrasse the transport was safely effected on a gradient of 10 per cent., until the military road was reached, when it was at once manifest that with a gradient of about 15 per cent. the load would be too heavy, so one of the 12-centimetre guns was left behind. The journey was then continued with some difficulty, as the steep road was in a rather bad condition.

It was apparent that the coal-supply would only suffice for the mountain journey, indeed it was quite exhausted about 1 kilometre below the Grossboden station. The second gun was then detached with the view of sending the engine back by itself. In turning round, the lead safety-bolt of the firebox melted and the fire was put out. The damage was repaired as soon as possible, a supply of coal and water obtained, and the return journey commenced.

At the commencement of the military road an 8·4 cm. gun-carriage was attached to the engine and drawn without difficulty to the end of it (over 4000 feet above the sea). The return journey to Andermatt called for no remark. The engine was then employed as a crane for loading the pieces of the armoured gun-carriage of the 12-centimetre howitzer.

The same engine was used between August 29 and September 21 in transporting heavy casemate armour-plates from the depôt at Göschenen for arming the defences at Galenhütte on the Furka. This was after it had been proved that it required a team of twenty horses, with much difficulty and loss of time, to transport a 6-ton armour-plate over the same ground; the expense was also considerable (about 800 francs per transport). As it was anticipated that, with the tourist season in full swing, the engine would meet many vehicles on the Furka Road, to prevent interruption of the traffic, sidings where the engine could wait as long as necessary had to be provided. Accidents, which were feared, did not happen, as it was invariably found to be easy to quiet horses which were restive at first sight of the engine, which was also not used at night. Very little damage was done to the road, only in some places where the rain had softened it the ground was turned up a little when the engine started after standing for some time.

Six armour plates, as well as various mantelets, girders, etc., of a total weight of about 43½ tons, were carried in six journeys within twenty-four days. This was after 8 pieces of a total weight of 22 tons had been transported by horses to the same place, also in seven journeys. The effective weight transported varied on the journeys from 4½ to 7⅓ tons, the gross weight between 7 and 10 tons (wagons 2½ tons, coal, tools, etc., half a ton); the distance covered was about 17 miles, with a difference in altitude between the two end stations of about 4600 feet, the steepest gradient being 9 per cent. (=1 in 11).

The pace averaged 4½ to 5 kilometres[1] per hour on roads with easy gradients (Andermatt to Realp), and on mountain roads with 8 to 9 per cent. gradients 3 to 3½ kilometres per hour without stoppages for watering or allowing other traffic to pass.

About 650 kilogrammes (=13½ cwt.) of coal, or about 24 lbs. per kilometre, were used, including the coal used in getting up steam.

On mountain roads the coal consumption averaged between 10 and 12 kilogrammes (22 to 26 lbs.) per kilometre, rising to 17 kilogrammes (37 lbs.) in bad weather. As only 200 kilogrammes (nearly 4 cwt.) could be carried on the tender, an additional 300 to 400 kilogrammes (5 to 7 cwt.) had to be carried on the other wagons, and small depôts were also made at Realp and Hôtel Galenstock.

Water for the engine was obtained from the numerous mountain streams along the route; where it was not easy to be got, supplies

[1] Kilometre = 1093·6 yards; 100 kilometres = 64 miles.

were stored in petroleum casks. The tender carried only 600 litres of water (132 gallons), so that on the mountain roads a fresh supply was required every 2 to 2½ kilometres, in the valleys every 3 to 4 kilometres. Watering occupied from 6 to 10 minutes.

The expense of the double journey was 217 francs; the cost with horse traction for about the same load being 792 francs.

English Experiments

A. *Extracts from the Report to the War Department*, 1858 [1]

The Bray Traction Engine. It works up to 8 (nominal) horse-power, and weighs 8 tons. A 68-pounder gun slung on a sling wagon, with ropes, levers, and tools of different kinds, was attached to the engine.

The engine started with this load of 7 tons on the 11th of May from the Royal Arsenal, Woolwich, up Burrage Road to Plumstead Common. The road is pretty steep, in several places the gradient being 1 in 10.

On the return journey to the Arsenal the engine and train were taken through Nightingale Valley, with a fall of 1 in 8. The pace downhill averaged 2·272 miles per hour, and appeared to be not less uphill. The coke consumption was 59 lbs.

On May 25 a second experiment was made, this time in drawing three 68-pounders and wagons; again steep roads with sharp turns were met with, but all went well.

On June 1 there was a third experiment. In this case a soft road had been specially prepared, made of shavings, sawdust, rubbish, etc., so that the wheels of the wagons attached to the engine sank in 17 inches, and often did not revolve but slid along, pushing the rubbish before them. The engine with its 8 tons of load got over 40 or 50 yards of this road when for fear

[1] Report to the War Department respecting the applicability of Bray's Improved Traction Engine, relative to the transport of heavy artillery.

FIG. 35.—Fowler Traction Engine and Train with Load of Wool as used in Australia.
(*See page* 58.)

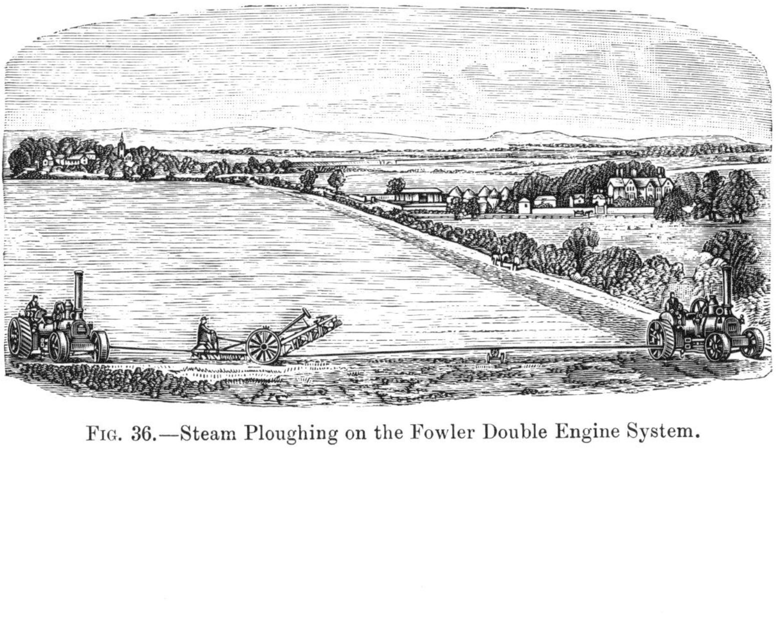

FIG. 36.—Steam Ploughing on the Fowler Double Engine System.

Fig. 37.—The Armoured Road Train telegraphed for by Lord Roberts.

Fig. 38.—Winding in the Limbers and Guns from a Hole.

of overtaxing it the attempt was abandoned. The engine was then tried over grass land with success.

The committee appointed to carry out the experiments had to report on the merits of the Bray engine, as compared with the Boydell engine used in the Crimean war. The report was to this effect:—

The chief difference in the engines consists in the different construction of the driving wheels. In theory the Boydell wheel is certainly the best. The broad flat under rails (see figs. 9 and 10) on which the wheels run prevent the engine sinking into the ground. But the system is not yet perfectly worked out, so that in practice it does not give the results which it might do.

Bray's engine on the other hand is better finished, and did its work without requiring to be repaired.

Both engines answer for different conditions. Boydell's is better for soft sandy ground, Bray's for hard and good roads.

As regards the cost of working as compared with animal traction, no decision can be arrived at without further experiments; but mechanical traction appears to be more economical.

When more perfectly constructed the engines may be suitable for use in India.

The committee then suggested that the engines should be employed in the Royal Arsenal, in order to gain useful experience for improved construction of such engines.

B. *Experiments at the siege operations at Chatham*, 1877[1]

These operations were concluded on July 27 in the presence of the commander-in-chief. The transport material used at this sham fight was quite modern; for instance, a tramway was laid down in one of the parallels for bringing up ammunition for the batteries. Great interest was shown in the traction engines, which with their loaded trains took part in the march past at the close of the manœuvres. On this occasion one 8 horse-power engine

[1] *The Times*, July 30, 1877.

drew three 32-pounders on trucks, and another engine of 6 horse-power drew two 12-pounders. Other traction engines drew wagons loaded with ammunition, baggage, etc.

C. *Use of the Traction Engine at the Berkshire Manœuvres,* 1893 [1]

At these manœuvres eight engines were employed, supplied by the following firms: Aveling-Porter, Fowler, and Howard. Only one of them (the Aveling-Porter) was new, all the others were older, some of them thirty years old. The engines transported 356 tons of supplies and camp material during the manœuvres from Aldershot to Ulfington, Idstone, Liddingstone, and to the various camping-places on the way. In spite of the age of the engines no accidents occurred, and the cost of the transport was extraordinarily cheap. The average cost for transport was a penny a mile per ton, as against twopence a mile with horse traction, a manifest saving in expense. The comparison would have been still more in favour of the traction engines, if engines specially constructed for military purposes with all the latest improvements had been available. As it was, most of the engines were built originally for agricultural purposes.

Some of the results obtained show what the engines can do in the way of getting over the ground quickly.

The 'Steam Sapper Queen' made the journey from Chatham to Aldershot, 72 miles (115 kilometres) in twenty-six hours, and resumed regular traction work next morning.

The 'Balloon' steam sapper, No. 24, drew 24 tons of freight to Idstone, 70 miles, in 30 hours, stopped there 8 hours, and then did another 22 miles to Aldershot.

D. *Employment of the Traction Engine at the English Manœuvres at Salisbury in* 1898 [2]

The traction engine has been used for many years past in the English army, for transport of camp material, for supplying the

[1] See note 1 on p. 53.

[2] *Report on the Manœuvres held in the Neighbourhood of Salisbury, August and September* 1898: London, 1899.

daily requirements for the water-tanks, and in pumping water; also with the balloon corps. In the last manœuvres experiments in transport of loads by means of engines of recent construction appear to have been carried out. The commander-in-chief, Lord Wolseley's Report on the 1898 manœuvres contains only one reference to this matter, viz.:—

'The manœuvres show clearly that mechanical traction by means of traction engines is an efficient supplement to animal traction, especially in carrying supplies in rear of an army.'

Engines of latest construction are specially serviceable and able easily to draw four wagons with a total load of 25 tons up steep gradients, and moved easily wherever the ground was fairly hard.

The appendix to the Report, which is signed by the commanding officers on both sides, as well as by special service officers, contains but few references to the traction engines. Colonel Henry H. Settle, chief of the engineer staff with the southern army, complains that the engines told off for water-supply were of an obsolete pattern and often broke down. On the other hand, Colonel Arthur Mackworth, chief engineer of the northern army, reports very favourably of the services of the traction engines in pumping and water-supply work; he especially mentions with praise the engines provided by Messrs. Fowler & Co.

In England billeting soldiers is not encouraged, the troops at manœuvres being invariably formed into camps, which may remain for a considerable time in one place if necessary, but are also rapidly shifted if the tactical arrangements require it. The transport of the tents and other camping necessaries requires the employment of a great number of draught horses, whose work could admittedly be more economically done by engines.

A good water-supply is of the first importance in connection with all military encampments. The reports of the engineers on the measures taken to provide water-supply and the results therefore occupy a considerable space in the appendix to Lord

Wolseley's Report. Various ways of procuring a water-supply were employed. Filtered river water was often used for drinking purposes. The formation of reservoirs of water for the cavalry camps had to be done in a great variety of ways, but all the reports agree in ascribing the greatest utility in this respect to the traction engine. It fulfils here admirably the double duty of transporting camp baggage and material, and then as stationary power engine drawing water and pumping it up for use in the camps often situated in elevated positions.

A fresh impulse was given to the use of the traction engine for military purposes by the experience gained at these English manœuvres, in which it was repeatedly shown how unsatisfactory and unreliable baggage transport by means of hired vehicles is. In all the reports of these 1898 manœuvres complaints are made of the great length of the baggage and supply columns arising out of the insufficiency of the hired transport arrangements. At every bit of steep road it was almost invariably necessary to employ army horses to assist the hired teams. In consequence of the delays caused by this unsatisfactory service it was always late in the day before the troops got their baggage.

Lord Wolseley's Report, therefore, points out that something must be done in the direction of increasing the means of military transport; and although it is not said in so many words that recourse must be had to mechanical traction, the successful experiments carried out by its means in the English army clearly indicate whence the help must come.

Experiments in Germany

The trials of the two Fowler traction engines in the war of 1870 have already been referred to on pages 23 and 24. A full report will be found in the supplements 8 and 9 of the *Militär-Wochenblatt*, 1886. After the war these engines were sent to the Cologne Fortress Command, and are at present employed in steam ploughing at Halberstadt.

Since then road traction engines have only once been used for military purposes. In 1872 the firm of Gruson had to erect two armoured turrets at Metz, and hired a Fowler traction engine [1] for the purpose of getting the armour on to the heights near the town, as it could not be done by horse-power; this was effected by the engine without a halt, and it was then placed at the disposal of the military authorities at Metz for other experiments in transport. They were confined to some journeys on the exercise ground, of which details have not been published.

The Traction Engine in South Africa

The war in South Africa has opened up a new field of utility for the traction engine.

It is evident that mechanical traction must be specially valuable there, where the conditions of the country necessitate the use of draught oxen, and the supply columns become of almost impracticable length. As each wagon requires from ten to twenty pairs of oxen, the number of drivers must be large, and the troops detached for convoy duty proportionately numerous. But rinderpest and South African horse fever make it impossible to rely absolutely on animal traction in South Africa, especially as the horses have to be imported, and at the very commencement of the war recourse was had to mechanical traction, which was already in use at Aldershot, where the traction engine finds regular employment in peace time. But engines, as used by the army in England, are not altogether suited for the local requirements in South Africa, and Messrs. Fowler of Leeds received an order from the War Office to turn out traction engines suitable for use in South Africa. Fortunately the firm had already supplied engines for use in mining and agriculture to the Transvaal

[1] The Friedrich Krupp Gruson Works at Magdeburg-Buckau now possesses two Fowler traction engines, which are employed chiefly for the transport of 50-ton hardened steel armour sections.

and Orange Free State, and thus were well acquainted with all the requirements of transport by means of traction engines in this part of Africa. Already, in the spring of 1897, Messrs. Fowler had sent out a representative—Mr. Robinson—not only to sell engines, but to find out by personal experience what they could and could not do in Africa, and what was wanted in the way of improvement.

The Engineer for December 8, 1899 published a long and interesting account of Mr. Robinson's experiences, from which the following extracts are taken:—

Presidents Steyn and Kruger introduced to the Traction Engine

'I arrived in South Africa in the early part of 1897, when rinderpest was raging in that part of the world. Having had many years' experience with traction engines and steam ploughing machinery, at home and abroad, for my employers, John Fowler & Co., Limited, of the Steam Plough Works, Leeds, this firm sent me out specially to travel through South Africa and collect information with regard to the conditions under which the above class of machinery would have to work.

'On arriving in Cape Town, I went direct to Honeynest Kloof. I crossed the Free State border about three miles from Honeynest Kloof Station, and it was here where I first came into contact with the rules and regulations laid down for preventing the spread of rinderpest. I travelled in the Free State for some three weeks, arriving at Bloemfontein about the end of that time, where I had the pleasure of starting the first traction engine which turned wheel in that State. President Steyn kindly consented to go to the railway station, crack a bottle of champagne on the wheel of the engine, and made a speech in Dutch relative to traction engines and steam ploughs in his State. I may say that, during the time the engine was being erected at Bloemfontein, President

Fig. 39.—Getting a Gun into an Armoured Truck.

Fig. 40.—Armoured Engine extricating itself from a hole in a ploughed field.

Fig. 40*a*.—The Fowler Traction Engine for Lord Roberts's Armoured Road Train. *See page* 90.

Steyn granted me a very pleasant interview at the Presidency, and suggested that my firm should use their best endeavours to introduce their steam ploughing machinery into the Orange Free State. He said that one trait of the Dutch character was that they did not care to adopt any newfangled arrangements, from descriptions given in catalogues, newspapers, etc., but that with them seeing was believing. I showed President Steyn some photographs of our military traction engines, hauling big guns, and endeavoured to induce him to order one for the State Artillery. He did not fall in with this idea, and remarked that heavy artillery would be of little use to his Government at any time. Going back to the trial of the traction engine, Bloemfontein made a general holiday for this event. A military band played us through the town, and several of the Free State Mounted Police were in attendance to keep the crowd clear of the engine. The wagons not having arrived from England, I got six ox-wagons, and, by means of a length of wire rope fixed beneath them, connected the lot to the engine, using the dissel booms simply as rigid bars to keep the wagons from running into each other when going down steep gradients. On these wagons I had about thirty tons of coal in bags, and in addition to this about one hundred Boer farmers mounted the wagons, making probably another five or six tons. We ran the engine through the main streets of the town, and then, by special request, we crossed a very bad spruit outside the town, where President Steyn had driven in front of us to see us cross. Hundreds of the Boer population had assembled here to see us stick fast, as feeling was running very high at the time against everything English. We crossed this spruit in good style, without the least hitch, when the Boers assembled could not refrain from giving us a good cheer.

'A short time after leaving Bloemfontein I had the pleasure of meeting President Kruger at Pretoria. My meeting was special and arranged for the afternoon, which was a very unusual time to interview the President. The usual time for visitors to see him was from 5.30 to 7.30 A.M. I waited upon him at the Presidency, having with me a gentleman who could converse in Dutch. The President cross-examined me at some length with regard to the machinery turned out by my firm. Previous to my visit he had been down to the Transvaal border to inspect one of my firm's double-engine steam ploughing tackles, which appeared to astonish the old man by the amount of work it got through per day. With the President were six members of the Raad. My catalogue, as it was opened at each page, was handed to the President, who appeared to express his satisfaction in short grunts, and handed the catalogue round to each member present, when the next page was opened and the same thing gone through again until they had come to the end of the book. Evidently the members of the Raad present were farmers, as they were much taken with the steam plough shown in the catalogue, attached to a traction engine and hauled direct. They considered this to be the nearest approach to their ox-drawn ploughs; in fact, the President gave me a verbal order to send such a steam plough out for his own use. Although I consider nothing existing is able to compete with the double-engine system of steam ploughing, I must say here that I have done some very good work in the Transvaal on the open veldt, breaking in virgin land with one of my firm's compound traction engines and a direct-drawn plough. Where the farmers are too poor to purchase the larger set of tackle, a lot of work can be done by the direct-drawn plough. Where circumstances will admit of furrows 1000 yards long or more being cut, a considerable loss of time would result from turning in short lengths. Such an engine would, of course, be available for the other work on the farm also. After the veldt had once been broken in by steam power, the operations in following years by animal power would be much lighter.

'From the Transvaal I went to Kimberley, and spent some time in the city of diamonds, residing at Mr. Findlayson's Central Hotel there—a very comfortable place indeed, where every man from the Old Country is always made welcome. I had the pleasure of seeing several of my firm's double-engine steam ploughing tackles at work on the diamond fields harrowing the blue ground which is brought up from the mines and spread on the floors or fields to be disintegrated. Naturally I solicited an order for some more of this machinery, but was informed by the chief engineer that another set was on its way out from England.

'From Kimberley I went to Bulawayo. At the time of my visit the railway in course of construction ended at Palapye, in Khama's land. Messrs. Pauling kindly gave me permission to travel on their construction train from Mochundi to Palapye. Although I had to lie on a truck-load of steel sleepers with some dry grass, rugs, etc., this was a luxury compared with my after-experience travelling up in wagon from Palapye to Bulawayo. I spent some time in Bulawayo and district, residing at the Charter Hotel there.

'From Bulawayo I went to Salisbury, some 310 miles distance, and travelled with Mr. Zeederburg's coach—or, perhaps, I had better call it a wagon—carrying her Majesty's mails. On this journey we averaged about a mile and a quarter per hour continuous travelling night and day. This will give one some idea of the speed at which Her Majesty's mail rushes through Mashonaland. Frequently when crossing rivers the passengers had to dismount and assist the wagon over the passes or spruits. When travelling through this part of Africa to Mashonaland and Matabeleland, one gets the impression that the land is much better adapted for agricultural purposes than in the Transvaal or Orange Free State. For miles the track passes through high grass—in some places 6 feet and 8 feet high—and the country is also well wooded; but in other parts of Africa I have seen scarcity of water, and abundance of dust and sand appears to be the curse of the country. I may say that it was during the dry season when I went through this district. I spent some time in Salisbury and district.'

Mr. Robinson suggested several improvements in matters of detail to his firm, which have been adopted, including means of protection from dust storms, etc.

The Traction Engine in Uganda

In February 1898 the Crown Agents for the Colonies bought two engines for working twenty miles in front of the head of the Uganda Railway. The work these engines did was very satisfactory, and resulted in an order being placed with Fowler & Co. for two similar engines with certain modifications, which engines were sent out in March 1899. On August 12, 1898, the engineer reported that one of the first engines had done most satisfactory work. In July it travelled 344 miles, and transported all rations for the earthwork coolies, besides hauling out the heavy cast-iron cylinders that were used for culverts. It also hauled to the site the corrugated iron pipes used for temporary openings, and earthenware pipes, and, in addition, supplied water to coolies working between Derajani and Kibwasi. For this duty the engines had proved themselves very well suited, and, owing to the great losses in bullocks and mules, they have been of great assistance in advancing the work.

On the 9th September 1898 the engineer reported:—'The trial they have had during the last month has been very satisfactory, and I would now recommend that two more engines, with the equivalent wagons, should now be sent out.'

On the 6th October 1898 the engineer reported that the traction engines had proved 'most serviceable in sending up rations, etc., and moving the camp, and large bodies of men can now be kept 20 miles beyond railhead. One traction engine ran 202 miles in eighteen running days, and the second one 266 miles in twenty-two running days.'

The modifications above referred to, required for the second order, were increased tank capacity, dust covers, iron enclosed cab, for protection against branches of trees—for these engines work through the bush—petroleum firing apparatus, in addition to coal and wood firing, and a 15-cwt. Bollard crane and a 5-ton jib crane.

In August 1897 the firm delivered to Aldershot one of its latest road locomotives, fitted with spring gear on both hind and front wheels, and also fitted with three road-speeds, arranged by means of patent locking gear, so that only one speed can be put into gear at a time, and to carry sufficient water for a 12-mile run; the load, including engine, was to be 60 tons on ordinary roads. It was tried in the Long Valley at Aldershot, and passed all its tests satisfactorily. With this engine it was proved that stores could be taken from Aldershot to Salisbury Plain—a distance of about 60 miles—in a day. That it could easily travel at a rate of 8 miles an hour, and when necessary to get out of the way of troops at the rate of 12 miles an hour, and that at the slowest speed it dragged a gross load of 80 tons on the level, and would travel 17 miles without fresh supply of water.

The engine is also fitted with an independent donkey pump for either filling tanks, water troughs for horses, or its own boiler. It is also fitted with a water lift by which its own tanks or troughs or independent tanks can be filled. It was also used for driving centrifugal pumps and electric dynamos, and for travelling with a captive balloon. Three more engines of this type were supplied by the firm to Aldershot for the Army Service Corps in July and August 1898. Three more engines were ordered before the war broke out, for delivery in August and September 1899, also for the Army Service Corps, and were delivered up to time.

Engines Ordered for the War

When war appeared probable, eleven engines were ordered early in October 1899, for delivery by November 14. All these engines were sent in to time. Two of these were Army Service type; three were South African type; four were the largest traction and winding engines, made for ploughing. These last are fitted with cylinders 8 inches and 14 inches diameter by 14-inch stroke, and will easily give off 120 horse-power. They are fitted with horizontal drums, and 500 yards of $\frac{7}{8}$-inch wire rope on each drum. Two have, in addition, drums with 1000 yards of rope on each drum. They will be used for winding loads over rivers and swamps, and up precipitous places. They are also to pull the trenching plough, which cuts a furrow 30 inches deep on the solid, and 30 inches wide. This enormous work is done by putting a pulley on the plough and anchoring one end of the rope so that the pull on the plough is doubled. These ploughs are generally used for vine and tree planting. In the Transvaal they will be used for making shelter trenches, and also for making the ditches at each side on roads. Two of these ploughs were also supplied.

A Special Traction Engine sent to South Africa by the English War Office

In November 1899 the English War Office, recognising the value of the steam traction engine, sent out fifteen to the seat of war. [According to *The Engineer*, the number of engines shipped, or in course of shipment, up to November 27, was twenty-four; of these seventeen were made by John Fowler & Co., and seven by three other makers, J. & H. MacLaren, Charles Burrell & Sons, and Aveling & Porter.—TRANSLATOR.] A special traction engine detachment was formed under the command of Colonel Templer,[1] and among the engines taken out were, at his special suggestion, two steam trenching ploughs to be used for making

[1] It is, I believe, chiefly due to Colonel Templer that the great value of the steam traction engine is now fully recognised by our military authorities. All interested in this question should read the paper on 'War and Power Traction,' read by Brigadier-General J. H. A. Macdonald, C.B., at the dinner of the Automobile Club on April 21, 1900, Sir Francis Jeune in the chair. General Macdonald said that the brigade under his command was the first military unit to employ power traction in this country.—TRANSLATOR.

shelter trenches and ditches. When the transport *Denton Grange*, carrying ten Fowler engines and forty wagons, was wrecked on the Las Palmas coast (Canary Islands), the War Office at once ordered another lot to replace them, which were quickly supplied by the firm. The wrecked engines were afterwards fished up, and are now doing duty under Colonel Templer in South Africa.

Naturally the War Office is reticent as to the results of its experiments, and we have to fall back on reports of the war correspondents of the papers for information as to the doings of the traction engine corps; and from these it appears that the results in South Africa have been even more satisfactory than was anticipated. Mr. Bennett Burleigh, the well-known *Daily Telegraph* war correspondent, describing the passage of the Tugela by General Buller's army, says:[1]—

'It was a prolonged and desperate scramble to get the men and about 400 wagons and nondescript vehicles down the steep, slippery bank, through the waist-deep stream, and up the sticky opposite slopes. Three ox-wagons were run down into the river and converted into bridge-piers, planks being laid whereon part of the infantry were able to pass over dryshod, but the planks and footing were insecure in places, and it came to be like walking the greasy pole at Ramsgate aquatic sports, for numbers of Tommies went hurriedly into the water in the most diverse and eccentric manner, to the surprise of lots of people. The much-laughed-at score of Aldershot traction engines did not stick or flounder in the mud, but lumbered about, doing duty with comparative ease and considerable regularity. Their flanged grips upon the wheels gave them a sure bite of the ground, which in one or two places they churned up rather deeply. A by no means overladen ox-wagon stuck in the middle of Blaauw Kraus Drift, close to Frere Station. Eighty oxen were tried, and were unable to move the wagon an inch. It seemed as if the whole column must wait until the vehicle was carted off. A traction

[1] *The Daily Telegraph*, February 5, 1900.

engine was requisitioned to try its powers, the enormous span of cattle was taken away, and a steel hawser was passed from the engine and made fast to the dissel boom, then steam was turned on, and with snort and whir the steamer walked away with the wagon, conveying it some distance to a high and dry part of the roadway.'

Value and Use of Armoured Road Trains

Very recently armoured traction engines with armoured wagons have been sent to South Africa. The armour consists of steel plates sufficiently thick to protect the engines, etc., from the effect of mauser and shrapnel fire. The engines are of specially powerful construction, and the wheels broad enough to admit of transport, not only on roads, but anywhere where wheeled vehicles drawn by oxen can be employed.

As regards the value of armoured trains for supply columns opinions will differ. The French employed armoured railway trains at the siege of Paris in 1870, which took part in sorties against the besiegers on several occasions, but could not face the fire rapidly concentrated on them by the German field artillery, and were obliged, invariably, to retire to the protection of the fortifications. After this failure of the armoured train in actual war, it was noted with surprise in Germany that it reappeared at the commencement of the campaign in South Africa, and was prominently employed in reconnoitring work, and, under the special conditions of this campaign, has rendered decidedly valuable service. All the same it must be admitted that the use of armoured trains on rails, within the sphere of action of the enemy, is a very risky affair, as a single opponent has it in his power to seriously damage, or at least render useless for a time, this valuable war material, by pulling up rails or blowing up the line. But the conditions are decidedly different, and much more in favour of the armoured train, when it is used on roads with the traction engine. It is proposed to employ the armoured road

FIG. 40*b*.—Truck of the Fowler Armoured Road Train. *See page* 90.

Fig. 40*c*.—The Fowler Armoured Road Train ordered by Lord Roberts (showing how gun is hauled into the armoured truck by the engine). *See page* 92.

train for getting up the heavy guns which it has been found necessary to employ in addition to the field artillery against the fortified Boer positions. The traction engines are in this case not to be used coupled direct to the guns, but coupled to the traction trucks on which the guns with their carriages are loaded.

The steel plates on the wagons serve as protection against rain, dust, and sand storms, as well as against shot from small calibre weapons, whose power of penetration might otherwise explode the ammunition in its cases, and so put the guns out of action prematurely.

The guns having been brought to their positions, the armoured traction train is then available for other purposes. It has been suggested that it might be sent forward to positions near the enemy's defences to cover and assist the troops engaged in attacking them. With the inferiority in number of the Boer guns, the fire of which can be kept down by the superior fire of the British artillery, such an attempt is not hopeless. And a train not running on rails (which gives the artillerymen time to aim at it), is a more difficult moving target to hit.

The advantage of the armoured train lies, however, more in the fact that it does not require large bodies of men to be drawn from the fighting line for its protection against the attacks of small independent detachments of the enemy operating in the rear of the armies. A small force acting under protection of the armoured train itself which it is accompanying will suffice to drive off attacking parties, especially as it can use quick-firing guns from the armoured wagons. By using searchlights it is also possible to employ the armoured train for protection against night attacks, by selecting positions suitable for its use in this way. It is also conceivable that the armoured road train may be employed as a movable fort, which can be sent to important points, such, for instance, as bridges, threatened by flying columns or independent bodies of the enemy unaccompanied by artillery.

In any case the use of the armoured road train is a very interesting experiment, the results of which are awaited with the liveliest interest in military circles.

Lord Roberts and the Armoured Road Train

[Thanks to the courtesy of the proprietors of the *Daily Graphic*, which paper has devoted much space to the very important question of Mobility in War lately, I am able to add here a description and illustration of the armoured road train specially ordered by Lord Roberts for use in South Africa.—TRANSLATOR.]

MOBILITY IN WAR—AN ARMOURED ROAD TRAIN

(*From the* '*Daily Graphic*,' *May* 18, 1900.)

'In a series of articles recently published in the *Daily Graphic*, under the above heading, stress was laid on the services which the road locomotive was capable of rendering in war. It is satisfactory to know that the military authorities are fully alive to the importance of this modern method of traction, and are making arrangements for varied experiments with road engines. One of the most interesting of these experiments took place on Wednesday last at Leeds, in the presence of several War Office officials, an invited party of journalists, and the senior partners of Messrs. John Fowler & Co. This experiment was the outcome of an order from Lord Roberts himself, who, about a couple of months ago, telegraphed for a set of road engines and wagons sufficiently armoured to withstand rifle fire, and sufficiently powerful to draw a couple of heavy guns, with their crews and ammunition. Apparently Lord Roberts's idea is that occasions might arise where it would be desirable to send forward guns, with a small escort, over a partially protected route. By making the engine and wagons bullet-proof, the whole train would be rendered safe against the attack of any raiding party unsupported by artillery. At any rate, the train has been designed and built, and, from a mechanical point of view, is a complete success.

A SPRING-MOUNTED ENGINE

'What may be called the basis of the design is the well-known road locomotive of Messrs. Fowler & Co. Engines of this type have already done excellent service in South Africa—some of them after two months' immersion in salt water. The most important feature of this engine is the manner in which it is suspended on springs so as to render a high speed possible without shaking the engine to pieces. This essential feature is in no way interfered with by the addition of armour, but a few minor modifications have been necessary in order to bring all the working parts within the protection of the armour plates. As the engine is now constructed, the driver, sitting within the safe shelter of an armoured cabin, is able to reach every necessary valve and to lubricate every part of the engine. Moreover, the armour-plates are so attached that they can easily be removed, if the military conditions should make it unnecessary to burden the engines with the weight of armour.

A GENERAL CARRIER

'For the design of the wagons credit belongs to the War Office itself, and especially to Captain Nugent, who is responsible for an ingenious contrivance, which enables the loopholes to be opened partially or completely, or to be entirely closed, as the momentary conditions of a fight may require. Another excellent feature of the wagons, also due to Captain Nugent, is the insertion of strips of leather between the joints of the steel plates, so as to diminish vibration. This addition may prove of very great value in action, by reducing, to some extent, the hideous and nerve-destroying din caused by bullets striking the sides of the train. The most obviously new feature, however, about these wagons is the arrangement by which the sides can be either opened upwards or closed inwards, according to the purpose for which the wagon is being used. If men are to occupy the wagon the sides are fixed in a vertical position, like the sides of a cattle truck, and the top is open to the sky. If, on the other hand, ammunition is to be carried, the sides can be bent inwards about a hinge till they meet, thus forming a complete cover, both bullet-proof and rain-proof. This adaptability of the wagon adds extremely little to the weight, but adds greatly to the facility of making up a train. The new armoured wagon may, in fact, be described as a "general carrier." It will carry men or ammunition, food supplies, or even the guns themselves.

PLACING A GUN IN THE TRUCK

'One of the incidents of the trial on Wednesday was a demonstration of the ease with which a 6-inch howitzer could be run up, carriage and all, into the armoured truck. Normally, no doubt, the howitzers or other heavy guns would be dragged behind the wagons as they were when the train started from Leeds. But in case of very rough ground being met with, or in case it was desirable for any reason to shorten the length of the train, the possibility of placing the gun and its carriage inside the truck might prove valuable. The process is very simple. Two steel rails, of a special design, which are carried for the purpose, are temporarily hitched to the end of the wagon so as to form an incline. The gun, with its carriage, is then drawn up this incline by a cable from the winding-drum of the engine. If necessary a 4·7-inch naval gun could be carried in the truck or wagon as easily as the 6-inch howitzer, only as the naval gun is so much longer its snout would slightly protrude from the end of the wagon.

A COUNTRY JAUNT

'A practical question of some importance to Tommy Atkins is the kind of travelling which he may expect to find inside an armoured road wagon, and this point was tested pretty thoroughly on Wednesday over the Yorkshire roads. For nearly twenty miles altogether the train steamed, at varying speeds, along the roads and lanes lying between Leeds and Pontefract, and at times one felt strongly impressed with the sense of incongruity at the contrast between this moving mass of metal and the peaceful rural surroundings. It must be frankly confessed that Messrs. Fowler's new safety-boxes are less pleasant for the purposes of locomotion than the comfortable restaurant cars of the Great Northern Railway, in which the party had previously run down to Leeds. In spite of the springs, there is necessarily a good deal of vibration when such a heavy mass of metal is advancing at the rate of six or seven miles an hour over hard macadam roads. But the vibration was, at any rate, not serious enough to prevent the scribbling of an occasional note, while, by watching his chances, your artist was even able to add a few touches to his drawings. The route selected for the trial had been specially chosen, because it offered a considerable variety of gradients. One long hill ascended was marked at the top with a caution to cyclists, but the road locomotive, with three heavy wagons and two howitzer guns, mounted the hill without any apparent difficulty. A long descent, some miles further on, gave an opportunity of testing the brake-power, which appeared to be ample for any purpose. The steering of the train was sharply tested at the entrance to the pretty little village of Oulton, where an acute angle was turned with perfect ease, each wagon keeping accurately to the line taken by its leader. A pause of some minutes in the centre of the village gave the local residents a chance of inspecting the new monster at close quarters, and one of the wagons was quickly filled with a laughing crew of women and children.

FACILIS DESCENSUS, ETC.

'The final test was to try the engine on soft ground. An accommodating farmer, with a due sense of patriotism, had given permission for the train to be tried over one of his fields lying in fallow. Very neatly the great armoured engine, with her long tail of wagons, was steered between the gate-posts, without touching either, and advanced boldly into the field. The slope was favourable and the running was at first easy. But the return was another matter. The driving-wheels of the engine—seven feet in diameter and two feet broad—were fitted with projecting ridges to give them a grip of moderately soft ground. But the ground in the field was too soft, and the great wheels slipped round and round, churning up the loose earth, and making no progress. To increase their holding, "spuds," carried for the purpose, were clamped on to the wheels, but even with this addition the engine only succeeded in digging deeper into the ground, and was still unable to move forward. The soft earth gave way at each revolution of the wheel. It was evident the load was too heavy for such an awkward piece of ground. The engine was therefore cast loose from the trucks, and, thus relieved of her load, easily mounted the hill. She then uncoiled her cable, the end of which was made fast to the trucks, and as the cable was wound up, the trucks and guns followed unresistingly. The difficulty had been overcome. Had it been even more serious, had the slope been so steep and the ground so soft that the engine, even without a load, could not have crawled forward, the driver would still not have been baffled. It would only have been necessary to carry the cable ahead and fix the end to an anchor—always carried for the purpose—and then the engine, by winding the cable on the drum, would have hauled herself up the slope, and then hauled the trucks after her.

IMPERVIOUS TO BULLETS

'The tests, therefore, proved in every way satisfactory, and the trains, with one or two trivial alterations of detail, will be promptly despatched to South Africa. The complete order comprises six engines and twenty-four wagons. The armour, it should be added, consists of steel plates a quarter of an inch thick, specially hardened by the Cammell process. The plates will resist direct rifle fire at twenty yards, and are impervious to shrapnel or splinters of shell. Needless to say, however, they will not stand direct shell fire. Exactly to what purpose the train will be put is

Fig. 40*d*.—General View of the Fowler Armoured Road Train. *See page* 90.

FIG. 41.—Traction Engine employed in pulling down and removing trees in front of fortifications, etc.

still largely a matter of conjecture, but it is interesting to know that a mechanical problem of some difficulty has been solved, and that Lord Roberts will soon have under his command six well-armoured trains capable of following any ordinary road, or of striking boldly across the veldt.'

The Traction Engine not at present used for War Purposes in the United States

Wishing to ascertain if the Traction Engine had been employed in war time by the Americans, I wrote to Captain A. T. Mahan to ask him if he would be good enough to make inquiries on the subject for me, and he very kindly replied as follows:—

NEW YORK, *April* 24, 1900.

'MY DEAR MR. MARSTON,—The enclosed is from our chief engineer officer, who served through the Civil War, and is in every way able to get any knowledge in the possession of our War Department. In haste to catch mail.—Sincerely yours,

A. T. MAHAN.'

OFFICE OF THE CHIEF OF ENGINEERS,
UNITED STATES ARMY,
WASHINGTON, *April* 21, 1900.

'Captain A. T. Mahan.

'MY DEAR CAPTAIN,—I beg to acknowledge the receipt of your letter of the 15th instant, making inquiry relative to the use of road traction engines in war by the armies of the United States.

'In reply I have to state that I am not aware of any instance of the use of road traction engines by our military forces, nor can any record of such use be furnished by the Commandant of the U.S. Engineer School at Willets Point, to whom the subject was referred for report. So far as I can learn, road traction engines have never been seriously considered as a means of army transportation by any Department of our Government, probably because the want of good roads in the countries where our military operations have heretofore been carried out preclude their successful operation.—Very respectfully, JOHN M. WILSON,

Brig.-Gen., Chief of Engineers,
U.S. Army.'

The Thousand Miles Motor Trial

(*April* 23 *to May* 12, 1900)

MR. BALFOUR'S DREAM

'In the House of Commons on Thursday evening, May 17, 1900, Mr. Balfour said he sometimes dreamed, perhaps it was only a dream, that in addition to railways and tramways we might see great highways constructed for rapid motor traffic, and confined to motor traffic, which would have the immense advantage, if it could be practicable, of taking the workman from door to door, which no tramcar and no railway could do. Is it possible for Mr. Balfour's dream to be realised? A representative of a firm of automobile manufacturers told a *Daily Mail* representative yesterday that in another ten years the idea would be feasible if the rate of progress made in motor cars during the past four years was maintained.'—*Pall Mall Gazette.*

No one who has followed the accounts recently published of the great motor car trial can have much doubt about the realisation, in the near future, of Mr. Balfour's dream. That trial has done more to open the eyes of the British public with respect to the present and future possibilities of mechanical motor road traffic than anything else in the whole history of the movement; and that history dates back more than a hundred years, as will be seen by a glance at the introductory part of this work.

I should like to have given the official report of the trial, but as that will not be published in time to enable me to do so, I have obtained Mr. Alfred C. Harmsworth's permission to reprint the *Daily Mail*'s general summing-up of the 1000 miles tour. Mr.

Harmsworth was one of the first Englishmen to pay serious attention to the subject, and certainly no one has done more than he has to make automobilism popular in this country, and no one regrets more than he does that British inventors and manufacturers have allowed their Continental rivals not merely to outdistance them, but practically to monopolise the field as regards the lighter forms of automobilism. In the department of mechanical traction on roads, especially where it is a question of transport of heavy loads, our manufacturers are still well to the front, but even here it seems probable that steam will find a more formidable rival in petrol and other motive powers than is at present the case. For instance, Mr. Harmsworth, who has travelled thousands of miles in France on his motor car, tells me that automobiles are far more extensively used in the French army for the transport of field guns and supply than is generally supposed. As recently as May 19th the *Daily Mail* published an account of a remarkable feat by a French automotorist which is significant indeed as regards the employment of motor cars in future warfare. The Uhlans of the future will certainly not always ride horses.—TRANSLATOR.

Forty-seven Miles an Hour

'Henri Beconnais, the king of chauffeurs, set up a remarkable world's record for 100 kilometres (about sixty-two miles) on Thursday last on the Étampes-Ablis (France) road.

'Profiting by the presence of the official timekeeper for the voiturette race won by Cottereau in 1 hr. 44 min. 57$\frac{3}{5}$ sec. over the same course, Beconnais on his motor tricycle covered the distance in 1 hr. 18 min. 57 sec., riding at an average of over forty-seven miles an hour, and beating his own previous record by about four minutes.'—*Daily Mail*, May 19, 1900.

General Summing-up of the Thousand Miles Tour

(*Daily Mail, May* 16, 1900.)

'It cannot, I think, be denied that the thousand miles motor tour accomplished all that was expected by those responsible for its conception.

'Through the medium of the Press, and by ocular demonstration, automobilism is ten times more of a reality to the people of this country than it was a month ago. The records of each day's run were closely followed by all sorts and conditions of men from one end of the kingdom to the other, so that it is not surprising to find altogether unlikely people fully acquainted with and interested in the performances of the different vehicles. From all points of view the tour really has done even more than was originally expected.

THE VICTORY OF PETROL

'It is too soon yet to allot positions of merit to the competing cars; indeed, that, I fancy, will prove a trying task to the fifteen devoted gentlemen who are now engaged upon it. But the broad issues are plain to the intelligent observer.

'One of them is the undoubted victory of petroleum spirit as the motive force for self-propelled road vehicles over all other agents. It may be said that steam was not well represented, but the world can only judge by what it sees, and the show made by the two steam cars that ran did not at any time suggest the displacement of petrol.

'Of the sixty-two petrol vehicles that left Hyde Park Corner on April 23, forty-seven registered at the Automobile Club in Whitehall Court on Saturday evening, and are on exhibition at the Crystal Palace.

'One of the chief officials of the Automobile Club informed a *Daily Mail* representative that electric motors—which have neither vibration nor smell, and are therefore preferable—are at present impossible for long distances. They require charging about every thirty miles. If stations could be established on the main roads, supplying standard batteries, electric motors would be all right.

'He added that, as the result of the exhibitions held in various towns, several hundred pounds will be handed over to the war funds.

'As I have suggested, it is necessary to wait for the judges' report before forming conclusions, but taking the running of the vehicles throughout, I think the Hon. C. S. Rolls's 12 h.p. Panhard and Mr. Edward Kennard's 8 h.p. Napier may be bracketed as the best vehicles of their class running in the competition.

'It should not be forgotten that both these cars, similarly, indeed, to all the petrol cars, were day by day, from start to finish, driven, as may be said, under forced draught, irrespective altogether of gradients or road surfaces, which in some parts south and north of Manchester, and in Yorkshire particularly, were trying enough.

'Emulation increased the severity of the trial quite 50 per cent. Notwithstanding this, no serious breakdown occurred to any but the experimental cars. Those who recall the story of the run to Brighton on Motor Day three years ago must therefore admit the extraordinary progress that has been made.

BEHAVIOUR OF THE VOITURETTES

'Intending automobilists who contemplate the purchase of small cars may like to know that the De Dions, the New Orleans, the Gladiator Voiturette, the Star, and the M.C.C. Triumph all did remarkably well, considering the severity of the test.

'One of the De Dions and the Star met with a mishap, but they successfully completed the round. It must not be forgotten that what was play to the high-powered cars was a very serious matter to vehicles depending for their propulsion upon motors of 3 h.p. to 3½ h.p. Therefore they are quite dependable for average use.

IMMUNITY FROM ACCIDENT

'If the Thousand Miles Trial has done nothing more than demonstrate the wonderful control and facile conduct of self-propelled vehicles, a great result may be said to have been achieved.

'Here we had fifty cars running day after day, totalling in all 52,950 miles, some considerable portion of the mileage being through crowded streets, where the eager spectators left but the narrowest passage for the vehicles, and excited children frequently darted across the road right under the wheels, without a single accident of any kind due to the driving or failure of the automobiles.

'I have heard of two accidents caused by frightened horses, but these regrettable incidents cannot be laid at the door of the autocar. Simply, the education of the horse has been neglected. Moreover, in the course of the tour the cars descended numerous hills steep enough to merit danger-boards being erected at their summits, and negotiated all manners of sharp and awkward turns, at times over very greasy and slippery surfaces, all without any mishap whatever. Like the Cunarders, they never lost a passenger.

'Whatever may be the future attitude of the police towards automobilism, the various county and borough forces all along the route, with two exceptions, spared no pains whatever to ensure the success of the undertaking. They posted themselves at the tops of steep hills and at difficult bends; they restrained the eagerness of the village and urban populations; in fact, they assisted to the utmost of their ability in every possible manner. The Automobile Club and all who took part in the trial owe the police a hearty debt of gratitude.

PUBLIC SERVICE CARS WANTED

'At the different towns visited in the course of the tour many inquiries were made by persons interested in the excursion business as to the possibility of obtaining vehicles for passenger transport, and it is regrettable that more satisfactory replies could not be made to such inquirers.

'The managing director of a company that does a large business in carrying excursionists from Sheffield to numerous points of interest within a radius of twenty-five miles of that murky city assured me that his company would drop horse haulage at once if they could be assured that they could carry as cheaply by motor vehicle. And this because they would be able, by changing the body of the vehicles, to earn money with their motors in winter time by handling goods, or if this did not prove desirable, the motors could stand idle during the off season at much less cost than horseflesh.

'There is a big chance for autocar manufacturers in this direction. Public service vehicles built on the lines of the ordinary car cannot be run at a profit.

FUTURE TESTS

'It is not likely that such a test as that which was so successfully completed on Saturday last will be repeated. The expense to the manufacturer is considerable, and one that he is likely to object to incur annually.

'But a test of 1000 miles to be run in six days of thirteen hours each would be even more severe upon the vehicles, and if an impartial observer went through on each vehicle the test would be more acceptable.'

Major Crompton's Electric Train and Cyclist Telephone Corps

'The electric train which Major Crompton has taken out to South Africa is intended to serve two purposes. In the first place the powerful road engines which form the most prominent feature of the train will be utilised to generate the electricity for searchlights, and in the second place the cyclists will be utilised to lay telephone wires. The machines ridden are specially constructed for this purpose. At the back of the saddle is a small drum on which the wire is coiled, and as fast as the cyclist rides, so fast is wire paid out and laid upon the road. The wire is bare copper wire, and in order to make a circuit two cyclists start together, one on each side of the road. When the wires have served their purpose and require to be moved to another place, they can be picked up by the machines at the rate of about four miles an hour. Each machine carries four miles of wire. These figures show that on only a moderately good road a party of cyclist electricians should be able to lay twenty miles of telephone wire in about two hours. The necessary instruments—namely, the receiver and the sender—are carried by the cyclists on their back. The road engines, as already mentioned, are required to generate electricity, but they have another and equally important function, namely, to convey the material for the electrical party—wire, dynamos, search-lights, reflectors, etc. The engines are employed for this purpose, not only because they are also serviceable for working dynamos, but because Major Crompton, after more than twenty years' experience of what a road engine will do, would not consent to go back to animal traction. One significant illustration of the superiority of the road engine has been recently communicated to the *Daily Graphic* by the War Office. Among the engines now working in South Africa are three or four that were wrecked at the beginning of the war, and have spent two months at the bottom of the sea. They were fished up and cleaned, and are now working with admirable efficiency, and as well as if they had suffered no mishap of any kind. The bodies of the horses that went down at the same time are officially reported to be not worth recovering.'—*Daily Graphic, May* 9, 1900.

The Traction Engine in the Navy

[Although this work deals chiefly with the question of the employment of the traction engine by the army, it seems to me to be probable that our naval officers may before long find the traction engine, with crane and wire drum, an indispensable part of their equipment for landing and transporting guns, etc., in such operations as those carried out by the Naval Brigade in South Africa recently, especially in cases where no railway already exists.—TRANSLATOR.]